MW01520079

Sing, Dance, Pray

A Collection of Prose and Poetry For Life's Journey

Joanne Daggett

Dance in His light

♡ *Joanne Daggett*

Copyright © 2022 Joanne Daggett

All rights reserved. No part of this book may be used or reproduced, stored in a retrieval system, or transmitted in any form or by any means, electronic, mechanical, photocopying, recording, scanning or otherwise, without written permission from the publisher. Permission for wider usage of the material can be obtained through Joppa House Publishing by emailing permission@joppahousepublishing.com

All Scripture quotations, unless otherwise indicated, are taken from the Holy Bible, New International Version®, NIV®. Copyright ©1973, 1978, 1984, 2011 by Biblica, Inc.™ Used by permission of Zondervan. All rights reserved worldwide. www.zondervan.comThe "NIV" and "New International Version" are trademarks registered in the United States Patent and Trademark Office by Biblica, Inc.™

Scripture quotations marked (GNT) are from the Good News Translation in Today's English Version- Second Edition Copyright © 1992 by American Bible Society. Used by Permission.

Scripture quotations marked NLT are taken from the *Holy Bible*, New Living Translation, Copyright © 1996, 2004, 2015 by Tyndale House Foundation. Used by permission of Tyndale House Publishers, Inc., Carol Stream, Illinois 60188. All rights reserved.

ISBN: 979-8-9872117-1-7

Cover design and layout by Anna Rhea | joppahousepublishing.com

Interior design by Ink Drinker Editing and Literary Services | inkdrinkerliterary.com

First Edition

Joppa House Publishing

annarhea@joppahousepublishing.com

https://joppahousepublishing.com/

Endorsements for
Sing, Dance, Pray

"Joanne Daggett is a poet, even when she writes prose. She captures deep feelings of grief, contentment, and joy with memorable words and pictures. If their impact on my heart is any indication, her words will help to heal your hurts and point you to our faithful God. You will be grateful that Joanne has let you into her life through her words. "

Stephen J. Lennox, Ph.D, President, Kingswood University, New Brunswick, Canada.

"Joanne's writing is deeply personal, refreshingly honest and profoundly poignant. If you don't know her before you read this book, you will most certainly know her by the end as she shares stories that range from intense joy to deep sorrow with captivating, remarkable strength and boundless courage. Joanne takes you on a beautiful journey through the ups and downs of life, making you cry, laugh, and be filled with gratitude for the Saviour who is beside us through it all."

Melanie Ingersoll, nurse and the lead pastor's wife at Kings Church, New Brunswick, Canada

"Joanne is a gifted and inspiring writer. No fluff here at all as her compelling words strike deep in your heart and soul. Read, reflect, then live out this message. You'll be glad you did."

Dr. Pete Benson (proud brother), author, speaker, co-owner of Beacon Capital Management, LLC

To Alex, for holding my hand, never giving up, and making me laugh along the journey. All my love.

Do you ever wonder how you ended up standing in the middle of your story?

Are there days you wish you could have a re-write, a do-over, another chance to choose a different path?

Does it sometimes seem so dark and formidable that you wonder if you will ever make your way back to the light?

You are not alone.

On the day our son was born, my 24-year-old husband was killed in a car accident on his way to see us in the hospital. At only 19, I became a mother and a widow and was left limping in the valley of a broken dream. Years later, I braced myself against the oncoming tornado that was my life—the loss of my parents, my second husband's chronic illness, a flailing business, and a child wandering on a prodigal's pathway. And now, while trying to navigate a path strewn with grief and fear, I watch my grown child struggle with addiction, crisis, and even incarceration.

Though darkness tries to win, His light has shone through the crevices and wounds of my sometimes-broken heart. My child-like faith has grown and strengthened as I stand in a posture of surrender and worship, even in the valley of the shadows. On a path marked with unknown and uncertainty, I know I can't go back, I can only walk forward with my hand in His, my Father, the Beautiful One.

He shines His light on me as I Sing, Dance, and Pray. Will you join me?

Contents

Con Dolore
(sing with sorrow)

STING
HEAVY DAYS
INTRUDER
SOMETIMES I CAN BARELY BREATHE
RAIN YOUR LOVE
HOLY BANDAGE
SALTY TEARS
AN UNCLEAR SURRENDERANCE
HIS KIND SHOULDER
WALKING IN CERTAIN UNCERTAINTIES
WRITING FROM HEARING
SOMEBODY'S SON
SLIPPERY SLOPE
HELP — I REFUSE
PAIN SAYS
ROADS UNNAVIGABLE
MOM
THE NEXT DAY FUNERAL
FIGHTING MY BATTLES
SOMETIMES, SOMEHOW
HOPE
HER FRIEND STOPPED BY
RAINY FUNERAL
A PRAYER FOR YET ANSWERED
ELIJAH, MY FRIEND
ELEPHANT SITS ON MY CHEST
BELIEVING
BE BRAVE
NO NEWS IS...

Facilimente
(sing with ease and without strain)

Cazonae Della Terra (sing with the earth and her songs) 194

INTRODUCTION

He asked me to dance, and I shyly said yes

A hesitant dancer was I

but I bravely said yes, stepped onto the floor

and trusted His steady strong hand

As I circled the floor

shame and doubt lifted

and fear lost its grip on me too

I looked in His eyes and saw love shining out

as I twirled midst the clouds of spring

In the intricate stepping, I saw summer float in

on a soft melodious breeze

with sunshine and beauty to warm my heart

we flitted through June and July

In time, our feet rarely missing a beat

we danced in the salty beach waves

Then I faltered a little as fall ushered in cooler days

with nostalgia and dread

His strong hand clasped mine and lifted my chin

Keep your eyes up, He tenderly said

So, the dancing continued through colorful fall

with golden and red leaves adorned

I trembled and tripped as December drew near

and He whispered

I am here tiny one

Into Advent we waltzed as the music grew strong

with the cadence

of hope peace and light

His beauty shone down on the darkest of days

'til Immanuel's birth graced the floor

Into January I bowed

with the unknowns swirling 'round

and the dancing was frozen like ice

But the touch of His hand

and the warmth of His smile said

We will dance

— always dance — keeping time.

There's healing in dancing

with my hand placed in His

There's music and rhythm and joy

He ushers it in as

we twirl across the floor

and we step to His story

and mine.

Music has always had a way of turning up the volume of God's voice in my life. Whether it's dancing on my tiptoes in the kitchen or raising my arms and voice high in the pews, all worldly noise fades away when the music starts to play.

Sure, sometimes it's easier to sing and dance God's praises than others. But I've found that it is one's willingness to sing and dance through the spectrum of feelings that strengthen her faith. At least that has been the case for me.

Is that the case for you too?

Do you have a strong connection to music? Are you a fellow dancer? Do you love to sing or play a musical instrument? If so, then you probably know about "style markings." I'm not talking about the notes or key signatures, but the style markings that tell you what emotion to portray through your voice, instrument, or moves.

Similar to these markings atop the staff on sheet music, there are times when it's necessary to sing with joy (*Gioioso*), to sing with sorrow (*Con Dolore*), to sing with ease and without strain, (*Facilmente*) and (for the sake of theme) to sing with the earth and her song (*Canzone Della Terra*).

All times call for praise as God is always present and faithful.

As I was curating these moments of prose and poetry for you, I figured that organizing this book according to these four specific style markings would benefit your reading experience.

Before we go any further though, let's check in to make sure that this book is "in harmony" with you and how God is leading you because while I want to keep hanging out with you, I also don't want to waste your time.

This book is not for you:

- If you believe that when times get hard, God has abandoned us.

- If you feel that Jesus' love for you must be earned through works and deeds.

- If you prefer to read academic books instead of feeling all the feels or colorful poetry.

On the other hand, this book is totally for you:

- If you believe (or want to grow to believe) that in grief and in joy, God is equally at work for good.

- If you want to feel Jesus' deep, sacrificial love for you in a palpable way despite the hurtful choices of others.

- If you are ready to add colorful literature to your spiritual disciplines.

So whatdoya say? Shall we *volti subito* (turn the page at once)? (Yes, that is an *actual* musical stylistic marking!)

Before we do that though, please remember that I'm here and happy to connect outside of this book. Please reach out to me on

Instagram @joannewdaggett and Facebook at Joanne Daggett at any time.

From the first to final page, may this prayer of my friend, Heather, cover you as it has me.

I pray these words are an encouragement to you, lovely daughter of the King.

You, Dear Reader:

You are fierce,

You are brave,

You are beautiful,

A gift,

An inspiration,

A treasured friend,

As I watch you obediently

Push back the curtain that is

Your testimony I see God's glory radiantly

Shining through all the worn, ripped, tattered

fabric of your story with each tug.

He is reweaving all of the thread bared pieces into a beautiful

New cloak that He has you, His beloved daughter wrapped in.

Keep going, keep pushing, and relinquishing those dark

Life choking shreds that He may continue to use to add

To the fullness, grace and love HE sees you walking in.

I envision you draped in a breathtaking, glorious, brilliant long and flowing shimmering cloak

With lots of pink and light.

You are a small but mighty warrior indeed.

Happy Reading,

Joanne Daggett

GIOIOSO

(sing with joy)

OLD CHORUS

"Therefore, if anyone is in Christ, the new creation has come; the old has gone, the new is here!" 2 Corinthians 5:17

"See, I am doing a new thing...I am making a way in the wilderness and streams in the wasteland." Isaiah 43:19

Remember the old chorus we used to sing in church—back in the 70s—I think?

"Something Beautiful"[1]—yes, that sweet song.

I was a kid, maybe a teenager, when I belted the words—sitting beside my friends in the wooden pew.

Belva tickled the ivories, and Peter led the worship time. Golden times, cherished memories of a life growing up beneath the red roof of an old country church.

When I think back now—it seems even sweeter, simpler and easier somehow. I loved singing those old hymns and choruses.

"Victory in Jesus." "The Solid Rock." "It Is Well."

For some reason this chorus came to my mind recently and I started singing in the car.

"Something beautiful, something good, all my confusion He understood ...."—yes, He understands.

I can say it with assurance. That gives me sweet peace.

When I think He doesn't or can't possibly understand—He does.

He knows. He knows the trial that causes the confusion and pain.

"All I had to offer Him was brokenness and strife, but He made something beautiful out of my life."

When I was a teenager, I really didn't "get it" maybe. I guess I did in a way, but now—after living what I've lived, walking where I've walked—I see the truth of the song in a new way.

From the trenches I've handed him my brokenness—and He has gently, carefully, taken it and remolded the mess into something of beauty (hey, I'm still a work in progress).

Amazingly.

Incomprehensible at times.

But that's the truly wonderful thing about God—He can do that.

Turn a broken life into a beautiful treasure, His treasure.

Read that again my friend, we are His treasure.

It probably won't happen overnight, although I know there are awesome testimonies

of that happening.

It can take time. Lots of time.

And even some hard work, grit and yes, once again, surrender.

Surrender.

The laying it down so that He can in turn create a new and beautiful thing.

And the cool thing about that too is that it may not look at all like we thought it would.

We may not even recognize the "beautiful thing" for a while, but we will. Am I right?

He can bring beauty into a situation we never thought possible.

He makes beauty from ashes, turns mourning to dancing, makes dry bones into armies, and sets prisoners free.

He even "rains acorns" every now and then to remind a tired girl of His LOVE for her.

How GOOD He is!

In a million ways He IS GOOD.

Every day I will trust He is doing a new and beautiful thing in the chaos,

and I will sing of His goodness.

MY ANCHOR

Words can't describe it — the bond we share.

We've been walking hand in hand for 34 years

on this journey of life and love.

When I look at him and us

and think about what I could say —

a million words seem inadequate.

Webster's dictionary doesn't have enough adjectives to describe

my love for him.

My mind holds thousands of pictures

from over three decades of us — together.

And you know they say, "A picture is worth a thousand words."

Countless photo albums and iCloud photos hold pictures

that tell snippets of the story of our life together.

Two teens smiling, sitting on a 3-wheeler headed out for a mud run
on an island trail.

Me styling a perm, and he sporting a cool mullet standing together in his parents living room

for a Christmas photo.

Our two faces smiling silly in a Halloween photo at a youth group party.

Prom, graduation, concerts, birthdays, summertime — all captured in a Kodak snapshot.

Then in a twist of life events we were separated for a moment of time and then choreographed back together in a dance without words.

A whirling and twirling and blending of heart strings wrote a love song

and soon two young hearts were wearing a gown and a tux

on our August wedding day.

So, there were three of us. Then four. Then five.

We danced and spun, laughed and cried, limped and struggled

our way through 30 more years.

Never giving up, always believing that the love song still played as our background music

in the dance of life.

When I stumbled, he grabbed my hand firmly but gently.

When he faltered, I walked beside him, believing for the two of us.

On his down days, I marched upward.

On my low days, he made me laugh, even when I didn't want to.

We've stood together in hospital rooms, in funeral parlors,

at family weddings, and in a grand baby's nursery.

We've smiled wide on the mountaintops

and cried long in the dark valleys — united.

Sitting on the deck in the evening his lips speak what my mind is thinking

— proof of hearts in sync.

That's how the love song keeps singing, and playing, and twirling us 'round.

Heart strings melded and meshed into one beautifully strong melody.

With no beginning or end.

As 2022 stands before us, there's no one I'd rather walk, stumble,

fly, limp, laugh, sail,

or simply be with than him.

My anchor.

(He thinks I'm his anchor, but the truth is — he's mine.)

SISTER

Swirly damp fog lifts our hair as we walk side by side on Deep Cove beach —

the beach of our childhood memories.

A thousand pictures play on our mind's projector slides.

Children laughing, salty, with freckled faces and sunburned noses.

Our hearts lock together as we share memories of blackberry picking

and mom's apple jelly.

We laugh as our toes tiptoe in the frigid water.

Our feet ache but we wade in anyway.

In the misty fog we snap a picture — sisters

Sisters by blood — friends by choice.

Sweet choice.

Another walk along a sandy beach, saying hello to neighbors along the way.

Gelato and cappuccinos are savored on Newton's shaded back deck.

Sharing stories of grandkids, heartaches, and of family members

who live on only in our heart memories.

One of us buys a whale shaped cutting board, the other buys a lemon cranberry bread.

We watch the ferry glide around Swallowtail lighthouse

from red Adirondack chairs on her deck.

It's peaceful and sultry under the August sky.

Sisters share hats and clothes,

dreams and albums of favorite memories.

Our eyes speak a love language only siblings can know.

Our hearts hold hands as we sit together.

Sisters.

Prayers are whispered for each other in the still night.

Knit together by Blood,

washed in the Blood,

walking by the Blood of the Lamb.

Sisters.

REMEMBER

Beautiful One, when we don't know what to pray — pray for us.

You are the beautiful Interceder

We remember YOU and your faithfulness,

and ask for you to meet us — once again.

We remember how you delivered the Israelites —

deliver us from the Liar — again.

We remember your kindness and mercy to the woman at the well
—

show us mercy in our weakness today.

We remember the way you provided for Elijah when he hid in despair for his life,

Jehovah-Jireh, beautiful Provider — supply us with enough for today.

We remember Your amazing love shown

in the bloody walk to Calvary's cross — thank you,

THANK YOU

We remember the empty grave, discarded grave clothes,

and nail-scarred hands, and we bow in humble adoration

of your BEAUTY

Beautiful One, we remember,

with hearts surrendered and arms lifted high,

we remember...YOU.

WAVES

"Because you are my help I sing in the shadows of your wings. I cling to you; your right hand upholds me." Psalms 63:7-8 (Hallelujah)

Waves, I love.

Waves that lap softly on the beach, rolling over sand and pebbles.

I love the sound of that—coastal music. Music I can dance to, and it makes me feel alive. Gentle waves make me feel like I'm HOME.

Soothing—like sitting on the warm sand of Seal Cove beach.

Home "sweet, tiny village" home.

Even bigger, louder, crashing waves—bully waves—they speak of HOME, too.

Some of those bully waves, and of course gentler ones too, have rocked the ferry that takes me to my childhood island home. Huge waves thrashed a cruise ship we were "cruising" on years ago—not a sweet memory—but a memory locked in my head forever now.

The sounds and smells of waves—the ocean tides, salt and sand—fill me up inside. I'm an island girl after all, saltwater courses through my veins.

And then...there are waves that I don't enjoy so much, they knock me over sometimes with their ferocity and strength.

Waves of grief. Stinging, aching waves. Ugh.

Usually, they hit me by surprise and can leave me breathless on the floor. Like being sucker punched (not literally of course, but almost).

I hate that.

"They" say that grief comes in waves. But why—I don't know.

They also say that I shouldn't deny the wavy grief, or push it away, but let it come.

Ride it out.

Face the grief head on, work through it.

It helps process it. Ok.

Let the tears fall, and scream if I want.

Write. It. Down.

Doing it.

My counselor is a beautiful godly woman who has given me "tools." Tools that look like setting healthy boundaries, reframing thoughts, and walking through the hard to talk about issues. Issues that can cause this heart to ache and bleed. Counseling isn't a magic band aid, but it works, even when it's downright ugly. Trust me, I know! There is hope in the healing and JOY even in the middle of the fire.

I really don't love these waves.

I long for the soothing kind, the peaceful ones, the gentler, kinder ones. Yes. Someday, I think to myself, maybe the grief waves will still.

Oh please Lord, let it be so.

I know you hear me. It may be your prayer, too.

You know what I'm going to remind myself of, and you, too...the Beautiful Healer, holder of bottles of tears, He sits with me.

Holds my tiny hands—the scraped and tired hands of the common island girl.

He says He will never let go.

Never. Let. Go.

"For I am the Lord your God who takes hold of your right hand and says to you: Do not fear, I am with you."[1]

This verse speaks hope and comfort to my bleeding battered heart.

He says that I can find shelter from the waves and the storm under His wing.

A sheltered, safe, no-wave zone.

You are invited too.

And His smile, His tender eyes, tell me that I'm going to be OK. Fine. Well.

I take His hand, slip His gentle wing around me and wait.

Wait in Him—for the waves and storm to pass.

LIGHTHOUSE

"In the same way, let your light shine before others, that they may see your good deeds and glorify your Father in heaven." Matthew 5:16

"When Jesus spoke again to the people, he said, "I am the light of the world. Whoever follows me will never walk in darkness, but will have the light of life." John 8:12 (Amen and amen)

Saltwater flows through my veins.

Waves lapping on the shore is the coastal music to which my heart dances.

At my core, I'm an island girl.

Born and raised on Grand Manan, beside sandy beaches, rugged rocks, and the freezing bay of Fundy. The beach is my "home."

My childhood memories include afternoons with my friend by the water, fog rolling across the coastline, and pretty lighthouses leading the way. Watching over us island folk.

To many lighthouses have I pilgrimaged in my lifetime, like the famous one at Peggy's Cove, and weathered stately ones along the coasts of Maine and New Brunswick. My favorite lighthouse is the tall white one standing gracefully on the cliffs of Southern Head. It overlooks the bay and its light shines brightly, warning boaters of the rugged coastline.

Of course, there are others that I treasure like Long Eddy Point (or the Whistle) and the picturesque Swallowtail, which also mark island points. I'm not alone in my love for them as they attract hundreds of visitors each year.

(If you've never seen a breathtaking sunset at the Whistle–well, you should!)

Their beauty and strength appeal to us all. Protectors of sailors, cruisers, and strong rugged fishermen.

Many of the people that surrounded me as I grew up—family, friends, and countless community members are all, in a sense, "lighthouses."

Lovers of the Light.

Strong, faithful, true.

They help guide us along, lighting the pathway to the ultimate Lighthouse—Jesus.

Some of these beloved "lighthouses" no longer walk here, including my grandparents and parents, and oh, how I miss them.

I long to see their lights again and I know one day, I will.

In their absence, the baton of "light shining" is passed onto me.

The weight of it, I feel. I want to be like those tall lighthouses, standing strong in the surges of wind and storm.

Unshaken, unmovable, strong on a firm foundation.

Rend Collective sings a song called "My Lighthouse." Oh, its catchy folk tune, it makes me want to get up and dance a little. But the words? Oh, they are what really speak to me. Such truth!

"In my wrestling and in my doubts

In my failures You won't walk out

Your great love will lead me through

You are the peace in my troubled sea, oh oh

You are the peace in my troubled sea."[3]

I mean, wow! I don't know about you but those truths (and I know they are true) make me want to shout and smile and dance a jig. Just ask my husband, he will tell you about my "kitchen dancing" to worship songs! Hands in the air, smile as wide as the ocean...on some days.

Other days, maybe not.

The truth is, sure, I don't feel like dancing every day.

Some days are hard, and heavy and sad. I feel the weight of carrying loss, and grief and sometimes shame. Yes, shame. On these days my feet limp instead of dance, and my eyes leak tears.

My song is a lament, a heart broken cry.

You see, I've known the grief that comes with losing a loved one to death. The grief and pain from watching someone I love dearly wander and struggle, is also something that I know all too well. This kind of grief looks like addiction, homelessness, and crisis.

But my God—my Healer, my Redeemer—He holds me and heals me. In His kindness He speaks truth and hope over the grief and wrestling with shame. He offers hope to a seemingly hopeless situation—all my hope is in Him.

He is my "peace in the troubled seas."

So, as I journey through this life, I keep my eyes and heart fixed on Him, my faithful Savior, Guide, the beautiful Lighthouse. He gently leads me along to healing, hope, and freedom. Ultimately to home with Him—safe.

He wants me to shine His beautiful light, to help guide others coming behind me. Those watching and waiting for me to stand, shine and be a lighthouse on a Rock. I will shine His light- the most beautiful Light.

"This little light of mine, I'm gonna let it shine!" [4]

WALKING

"For the Lord is GOOD and his love endures forever; his faithfulness continues through all generations." *Psalms 100:5*

"Be joyful in hope, patient in affliction, faithful in prayer." *Romans 12:12*

I'm walking tonight and listening.

To the cardinals' song, the chickadees singing, and the gentle breeze.

It caresses my hair, soft.

The sun is hiding behind a few dark clouds, but it's there, I see a tiny shimmer on the river.

Peaceful.

Until a big red smelly dump truck interrupts it all.

Rude. Just doing its job — hardworking and pushy.

I grit my teeth until it passes by, leaving a stench as it rolls up the hill.

But soon, all is quiet, and I can hear my worship music again. "She" is singing one of my favorite songs, "Goodness of God."[5]

Yes!

The words lift me up, and my arm raises high.

Smiling, I sing.

Peace again settles on my being, my "fine" being, and I walk on.

I start to think about life, and hope — and walking in hope. Another song I hear reminds me of the hope that comes from knowing He walks with us through the trials of life - that He never leaves us alone.

It's good to sing these songs to ourselves — to myself.

To remind myself of His goodness and His hope.

Yes, HOPE.

Hallelujah, HOPE.

Hope that declares I am safe and held in His hands. Cared for and immeasurably loved.

You know, I don't know why we walk through fire that sears our hearts.

I wish the valleys weren't so low and the pain didn't cut so deep.

I wish some nights weren't so long, and that our hearts didn't limp — bleeding and aching.

I wish our feet weren't blistered and tired. Sore.

I wish we walked on easier trails, and paths marked only by beautiful views, rainbows and sunshine.

Of course, at times, it is like this, and I'm truly thankful.

But this I do know: I've seen beauty in the blood — in His broken heart — in a cross drenched with blood. Blood that should have been mine, yes. But His blood brought beauty to an ugly wooden cross.

Sin-washing blood!

Blood that heals scars, and mends lives and offers amazing peace.

He made discarded grave clothes and a lifeless cold tomb beautiful.

Beautiful Redeemer.

He is the beauty that walks with me, surrounds me, and carries me.

He makes my limping ugliness beautiful.

His eyes shone beauty when He extended his hand to a little girl in a little fishing village

and said "Daughter, you are forgiven."

He still looks at me — and you — that way.

I walk a beautiful trail, because I walk hand in hand with the beautiful One.

Hallelujah — I keep walking and singing of His goodness.

GRATITUDE

"But even if he does not, we want you to know, Your Majesty, that we will not serve your gods, or worship the image of gold you have set up." Daniel 3:18

"I will give thanks to you, Lord, with all my heart; I will tell of all your wonderful deeds." Psalms 9:1

She often asked her sister "How do I give thanks for EVERYTHING?"

It seemed too hard.

Not quite right.

She wrestled with it.

I mean, some things don't seem worthy of thanks. Like prison walls and tired feet — aching tired feet.

The aching, limping walking.

Oh, there was lots to be thankful for in the midst of the pain and grief.

Things like family and faith, home and health, and nature's beauty around her.

She'd been filling up gratitude journals for years, and they helped her see the beauty beyond,

and even *in* the muck.

She had painted a Bible verse onto a canvas that sat on a shelf reminding her to *"Rejoice always, pray continually, give thanks in all circumstances."*[6]

Give thanks for everything.

But the fragile state of her heart, the unanswered questions,

all kept her asking *"How Lord, how?"*

She prayed

and asked,

cried and wondered.

Now, as Fall ushers in a season of Thanksgiving, she ponders in her heart how to gently hold "thankfulness" when prayers hang unanswered — when there are empty seats at the dinner table — again.

And how to be thankful in the middle of the "waiting, wanting and weariness."

When "thankfulness" sits at the same pumpkin-adorned Thanksgiving table as "aching loss."

As the days, months, and years unfold she rests more in the HOPE of her Heavenly Father. She knows she can trust Him, even in the fear and grief — in the unknowing.

She is confident, not in "knowing"

but in "knowing Him."

He's held her this far — even in the fire.

Especially in the fire.

In His unfailing faithfulness and kindness, she rests.

She knows He holds it all

and is thankful.

Not for the trial necessarily — but for Him.

Thankful for His beautiful peaceful presence — for His hand securely holding hers.

"For I am the Lord your God who takes hold of your right hand and says to you: Do not fear; I will help you."[2]

She remembers a song she used to sing in church:

"Daily bread, give us daily bread,

bless our bodies, keep our children fed.

Fill our cups, then fill them up again tonight.

Wrap us up and warm us through,

tucked away beneath our sturdy roofs.

Let us slumber safe from danger's view this time.

Or maybe not, not today,

maybe You'll provide in other ways

and if that's the case...

We'll give thanks to you with gratitude,

a lesson learned to hunger after You.

That a starry sky offers a better view

if no roof is overhead,

and if we never taste that bread." [8]

And today, as she sits at her table with a few grey hairs, more wrinkles, and her grandchildren, she smiles and prays that she can embrace gratitude.

Even if she *never tastes that bread.*

Gratitude that sees the beauty He graciously, kindly, faithfully offers, even in the brokenness.

Beauty — even and especially in the brokenness.

Thankful — her heart sings it.

WHICH COMES FIRST?

"Yet I will rejoice in the Lord, I will be joyful in God my Savior."
Habakkuk 3:18

In the walking, and the waiting, in the striving and the struggle sometimes heaven seems silent. And the silence can be deafening.

Some days gray clouds hover over me with no words to ease the pain or grief or longings. Prayers rise from bended knees and yet no answers arrive at my door. There's no miraculous healing or pretty gift bearing just what I need or even want.

You know, that "thing" that would make life easier, more manageable, and more kind.

So, my heart is left to keep clinging to what I know is true, when truth is hard to see, and answers just don't rain down.

Jesus said, "I am the way the TRUTH and the life." So daily I cling to Him and lean on His every word. I do this as I read the Word, sing the Word, hear and obey the Word.

I walked through a difficult season many years ago, and truth is, most days my feet still walk on a similar path today. During that season life felt like it was coming unraveled, and it had left me feeling weary and down hearted.

I was entering an empty nest season (which isn't bad, of course) but, nonetheless, an adjustment for this mother-heart. I had recently said a final goodbye to my dad and was walking with my mom through the "long goodbye" of Alzheimer's disease. The business that my husband and I had poured over 20 years into was failing. My husband's health was like a roller coaster ride, twisty and unpredictable. Dealing with his unstable health and the side effects from his medication left him, and me, wondering what the next months, or years would look like. Also, there were the daily challenges this imposed on our family and business.

I remember I would wonder why my prayers didn't seem to produce the answers I wanted and needed.

I wondered why heaven and God seemed so very silent.

I'd ask *why* with tears pouring out of my eyes. I began to grow weary and discouraged.

Around this time my sister introduced me to a book by Ann Voskamp called *One Thousand Gifts*.[9] I picked it up, began reading, and started the daily practice of naming and recording His "gifts." Voskamp writes, "And I see it now for what this really is, this dare to write down one thousand things I love. It really is a dare to name all the ways that God loves me. The true Love Dare."

I wondered if it would be too hard in this season of waiting and wrestling, of mourning and meandering.

Would I have eyes to truly see the gifts from His hand all around me?

Turns out I did.

Over the next days, weeks, months, and, yes, years, I wrote down at least three gifts each day in my journal. I began looking for Him, and for His beauty in the gifts from His hand. Simple things like a good cup of coffee, a bright red cardinal singing a good morning melody to me, or the smile on a grandchild's face. Small things added up to pages and pages of a thousand gifts to be thankful for.

They were bountiful and beautiful, and I was never left empty handed. My eyes noticed, my fingers wrote them down and my heart agreed with them.

Gratitude became my attitude.

In the sacrifice of offering daily thanks, even in the hard, He offered His presence and communion. As I began to let go of things I couldn't control or fix, He filled me up with the joy of knowing His intimate care and love and goodness.

Oh, that had always been there because He is faithful.

The practice of writing His gifts down and looking beyond the mess for the miracles of beauty helped me grow in intimacy with my Abba.

Daddy. The One who never lets me down.

When my focus changed, my heart changed. When I practiced the discipline of "giving thanks" and offered the sacrifice of praise, He met me there and lifted me up. I started to see that the hope I was longing for is only found in communion with Him.

In leaning on Him and trusting in His goodness.

Ann Voskamp writes on her blog,

"Gratitude is not only a response to God in good times - it's ultimately the very will of God in hard times. Gratitude isn't only a celebration when good things happen. It's a declaration that God is good no matter what happens."[10]

Circumstances will always have a way of casting my eyes down, so I will remember to keep my eyes up, postured toward Him.

Arms up, hands open, heart surrendered in the trial, the grief, and in the walking and waiting.

As Voskamp says, "Being joyful isn't what makes you grateful, being grateful is what makes you joyful."

My joyful heart agrees with hers.

YES

This month marks a year of "saying yes"

to writing and sharing the words God gives me.

They truly are His words written through my story and pen.

It still amazes me that He uses what I offer to Him, and turns the writings

into God — honoring posts.

I read them over and over, these wordy treasures He has blessed me with.

I love that He plants His "love notes" in my heart's soil, and my pen writes

from the overflow of my heart — and His.

His words are a lifeline from my heart to His — a place of safety and protection

and unfathomable love.

For me, a little girl from a little island in the Bay of Fundy.

And they are for you, the readers, who read them and who encourage me and give glory to Him.

All to Him, all for Him, all through Him.

My pastor reminded us last Sunday

that as believers we receive so we can release.

My heart leapt with joy when I heard this because, although I have known it,

I needed to be reminded that as I receive words that I also need to share them.

His words are the treasure in the trials and I long to share the bounty.

My counselor also reminded me last week (Yes, I'm still going. Yes, I love her. I'm not ashamed.) that I'm to receive messages of encouragement as prophetic words.

God uses your words and comments to speak prophecy to me.

I love this and it is so true!

Two reminders in one week for this

hanging-onto-hope girl

to keep seeking, listening, writing and sharing.

I say yes.

INVITED

"He has sent me to proclaim freedom for the prisoners, and recovery of sight for the blind, to set the oppressed free," Luke 4:18

I used to belong to a club. A private club.

I didn't invite you. Or my husband. Or my friends.

It was a "me only" club.

I hated being in it.

It wasn't fun or creative like a crochet club. Or a book club. Or a hiking club. No.

It was an ugly place. It was a club I had created for "moms like me."

Moms who have a son in jail — again.

I didn't want to be in it. And yet, there I stood.

Alone. Isolated. Ashamed.

Tears flowed there. Angst crawled through my chest.

Fear crippled my walking.

Shame sneered insults at me.

It was my own prison.

God wanted to unlock the door and set me free.

"Daughter, I didn't choose this for you.

Come out and be free and dance in your God-given PURPOSE.

One that offers peace and life, freedom and JOY."

In one grace-filled motion He swung wide the door and I stepped into the LIGHT.

Truth spoken broke the chain of lies.

I laughed.

A smile stretched across my face.

My feet did a little dance.

You won't find me at that club anymore.

Shame offered no peace and life in its "club."

I don't live there anymore! Hallelujah for His freedom. His truth.

Jesus Christ my LIVING HOPE.

He sets the captives free.

INK

My daughters have tattoos.

My sister has one, and my son-in-law has a half-sleeve tattoo of antlers (and more).

My hubby talks of the one he wants to get.

But I'm not getting a tattoo.

You see, I like to say that I already have one.

You could look me all over (and how awkward would that be) and you won't find

a pretty meaningful tattoo

of a flower or an anchor.

You won't see it, but it's there...on the inside.

On my heart.

JESUS — His beautiful name is inked with blood across my heart.

He bought my heart with his life — His redeeming blood.

And in my little devotional book, Shannan Martin writes "Let Him heal you.

Then bear your scars as holy tattoos connecting you to the rest of His kingdom,

marking you as healed."[11]

Wow. This made me smile and even giggle.

I DO have tattoos, and they're holy!

Healing, holy spots — scars.

From trauma. And grief. And shame.

In the healing and the mending, holy scars remain.

He says they are beautiful because He is shaping them

into holy tattoos that bear witness, marking me as healed.

By the Healer — Jehovah-Rapha.

I've been tattooed by the greatest tattoo artist of all time.

Jehovah-Rapha.

Beautiful Healer.

I've been INKED!

RENEWAL

Lockdowns and restrictions

household bubbles

directional arrows

masking and social distancing

None of it feels like renewal

It feels restricting and isolating

and honestly a bit futile

especially two years into it

and in bitter cold January

So the renewal comes from within

like an afternoon walk with a river view

like breathing in deep breaths

like singing a worship song

with lifted hands and eyes and heart

Like a friend's voice on the other

end of the phone

Like faith that stubbornly holds onto hope

like a father's steady reminder

of His faithfulness and love

hope and peace

Yes, it's time to renew our minds

one day at a time

one step at a time

Renew my spirit dear Lord

WHISPERS ACROSS THE SKY

And just when I've given up hope

that the day would remain overcast

the sun breaks through.

And I look up.

Late afternoon clouds break away

to the sun

boldly shining

through my picture window.

A shimmering guest

lighting up the room with an amber glow.

Its brilliance illuminates my Christmas tree

like no string of lights ever could.

All is quiet

except for the majestic melody

of a thousand rays of sunshine.

Rays of SUNSHINE

that brilliantly announce

LIGHT

and HOPE

and JOY

on a dull November day.

And then slowly it slides behind the hill

leaving behind lavender

orange

grey

and blue hues

that testify to its lingering presence.

It makes me smile,

standing in the kitchen

stirring chicken soup.

Even the pewter river dances with muted rainbow colors.

Alive

The clouds and sky

and water and trees

sing: Look up!

Look to the Heavens —

there is beauty all around you.

I'm reminded of His presence

and beauty

and HOPE

even in the ordinary

dull

sometimes too grey days.

Look up

He speaks

He whispers across the sky

He declares as He paints a glowing kaleidoscope of colors

in the darkening sky.

December beckons from around

the corner

and He speaks

Look up, child.

I'm HERE.

I. AM. HERE.

I am the priceless gift of beauty

your heart is longing for.

Hoping for

Waiting for

Look up.

RIPE BEAUTY

"For he satisfies the thirsty and fills the hungry with good things." Psalm 107:9

"...every good and perfect gift is from above, coming down from the Father of the heavenly lights who does not change like shifting shadows." James 1:17

I noticed her on my afternoon walk.

At first, I glanced

and then I noticed

and I smiled.

Oh, I smiled BIG.

My camera snatched a quick picture or two, and I walked on.

I thought about her brilliant beauty,

so unexpected.

I mean, all her lupine friends had shown up for the dance,

the party,

the summer gala,

dressed in beautiful hues of purple, pink, white, and deep blue.

But that party ended in July

so why was she here

standing alone in a ditch?

So alone

and yet so tall and proudly wearing her royal-colored gown.

Did she not know it was now the last days of September?

Was she not ready back in July?

Maybe she lost her invitation?

Had she lost her way?

Never mind,

she was here now.

Unexpected, yet noticed.

Head held high, just "being."

Oh how I love her spunk and her willingness to show up in fall

instead of summer.

Her beauty is a gift to walkers who notice.

And these two raspberries

hanging onto a bush in late October?

They were late to the "berry party" as well.

Bowls of ripe sweet red raspberries were picked

and savored

and made into delicious desserts

back in August.

This pair could have gone unnoticed,

hanging there almost hidden by overgrown bushes

and a few leaves.

But their ripe beauty caught my eye, again.

And I noticed.

And I think about it,

the unexpected gift

of smile-widening beauty

and the eye-blinking surprise.

I wasn't looking for raspberries this cool morning

on the trail behind my house.

But there they were

clinging onto a bush,

reminding this tired girl of

hope

life

joy

and beauty.

A gift on a Saturday morning

or an ordinary walk —

from a loving Father

who loves surprising his daughter

with spectacular

beautiful

hope-giving

reminders of life.

Life

I'm keeping my eyes open to see the beauty

in unexpected

spaces

faces

and places.

Are you?

LET THE CURRENT

The quiet river invites us

and the evening sun still warm agrees there's time to dip a paddle

into the glassy water

and gaze into the turquoise sky

and rest

A time to lay aside a few burdens

they will wait for tomorrow

A time to relax the arms

and slowly let the current

move us along

listening for an eagle's cry

Watching for a lightning-quick silvery fish

jump for a tasty morsel

A time to let the sun's rays

warm our faces and hearts

hearts that some days

weigh us down with restlessness

A time to rest

from burdens that are too heavy

and from things we can't fix today

Yes, let's sit in our kayaks together

in the summer evening sunshine

on the peaceful quiet river

and rest.

FRAGRANCE OF HIS WORDS

I smile when I think about the words.

Words I didn't want to write.

Fear held me back.

Insecurity too.

Like "Why would my story matter?"

And honestly, I'm just too tired to write anything.

I like to read, not write. *sigh*

But I smile again and giggle a bit when I'm driving.

"God, you amaze me with your words. And your grace poured out in ink on a page." (They truly are His words.)

You see I fought the writing for a while. Just ask my hubby...and my counsellor.

Oh, they were so patient. They waited.

And God nudged and gently prodded me.

But the truth is, in the writing, I'm only the vessel. He is the beautiful wine being poured out.

He is the blessing in the "becoming."

Lord you are!

I've sung the songs about being poured out and offering my life as a vessel.

I know the words. I do.

I picture the vessel as being kind of plain looking. Nothing special on the outside.

Functional. Dependable. Sitting on a shelf ready for use.

Ready to be filled up and then poured out. Ah, a beautiful picture.

"Will you write?" He asks.

"Tell the story — My story?"

So, I say yes and open myself up, and let beautiful words fill up and then pour out.

Because in the telling HIS beauty is poured onto a page.

Like a fragrance of unimaginable worth.

Even in the plain — a marvelous filling.

I pour out my heart, my words, His words.

Fill me up Lord.

WHAT HE STARTED IN ME

"...being confident of this, that he who began a good work in you will carry it on to completion until the day of Christ Jesus." Phil 1:6

I like to think

I determine certain things

like the clothes I'll wear

the food I'll cook for supper

and if I'll walk 30 or 40 minutes.

34 years ago, I was determined to marry my husband

and we determined choices

for our life

where we would raise our family

and worship God

and walk a life together.

Certain things we couldn't determine

like why my husband would get sick

or that our daughter would marry

and raise her family

thousands of kilometers away

or that a son would walk a prodigal's pathway of crisis and struggle.

I have determined that my

Abba is faithful and kind

and good in a thousand beautiful ways.

I know He will never let go of my hand.

He is determined to finish

what He started in me.

I'm determinedly thankful.

HEALING REVEALED

A year of writing

of saying yes

and putting pen to words

A year of struggle, limping, grief

with a still-bleeding heart

They all sit with me

and fear still crawls into bed with me

some nights

And the aching longing still clings

like a leaf hanging onto a branch

in November

A year later and there's no pretty box

tied with a ribbon

holding the answer I've prayed for

No easier, gentler path to walk along

No looking-back-smile that says

"There, you made it through to the other side."

Safe and sound and all better

except for a few pinkish scars.

No — not like that.

A year of writing my journey, yes

but also, *years* of living the journey.

A trauma-filled, grief-laden, rocky-

uphill, and slippery trek.

In the unknowing mornings

and limp-walking days

there is also sunshine and beauty

and intimacy.

A "being known" and seen and heard, comforted and loved.

So loved

Lament opens my arms wide

and surrenders my heart longings

to my Father.

Arms up worship in my kitchen

prayers on my afternoon walk

and a hands-open posture embody

Surrender

That is my story a year into this

heart-sharing-vulnerability.

A vulnerability that reveals healed scars and not fragile wounds.

Yes, in the struggle there can still be healing, and I say Amen to that

Watching the river fog lift

on a cool March morning

with the ache still squeezing

I stand in a posture of worship and faith

With trust in my Abba

that He holds my tiny hand in His nail-scarred one.

His eyes still shine with the LIGHT

of His lovingkindness

His heart still beckons me to rest

and His hand still reaches out

to carry my too-heavy burdens.

His healing hands that offer *hope*

and *grace*

and unquenchable *love*.

For me — for you

I stand in Him.

ARMS UP AND HEAD BACK

Arms up

head back

hands reaching high

For heaven

Fingertips pointing

Eyes closed

A tiny smile

Maybe even a little twirl

Reaching

On tiptoe

For heaven

Like a young girl — reaching for her father

Daddy...

A posture that whispers hold me

Pick me up, please

Save me

Protect me

Love me

Abba

Arms open

heart open

eyes closed

Like a trusting child

Leaning into her Father — yes, leaning —

I wait and He answers

Every. Single. Time.

Here I am child

I'm here

You are safe

Loved

Protected

Cherished

Priceless

Bought with a price...

Holy ground in my kitchen

and on the beach

A *graceful* heavenly dance with my Father

Heart-healing

Child-like posture

Arms open wide

On tiptoe

Head back

heart wide open

A tiny smile

Reaching

Waiting...

Trusting

Receiving

CON DOLORE

(sing with sorrow)

STING

"The Lord is close to the brokenhearted and saves those who are crushed in spirit."

Psalm 34:18

I feel the sting of a hundred losses.

A thousand losses maybe — yes.

It's a stinging ache deep in my being.

I can't shake it even though I try

and desperately wish I could.

Of course, I pray too, asking for heavenly relief — holy bandages.

Photographic memories live in my head — swirling, twirling, scattered.

A scattered swirling of old photos and childhood faces that cause a tear

instead of a nostalgic smile.

I wish it was a smile — and I mourn the smile.

The shaky smile that hides behind a tear or two.

I peek between the pages of old albums and the faces of a thousand dreams stare back at me.

Dreams that once beat strong in this mother's heart.

What can I do with the broken ones?

I don't know.

I'm not sure how to hold the broken ones and the beautiful ones together, at the same time.

It seems impossible and heavy.

My hands and heart can't possibly hold both, can they?

Maybe if I mix them together, the colors of the vivid dreams will bring a kind of beauty to the grey ones?

Maybe?

It's possible...

To smile through tears and hold all the memories like a precious gem

or a priceless treasure?

Yes, Father?

Yes, Healer of all the broken things - like dreams -and lives?

And so, for the millionth time it seems,

I lay it all down.

Because this girl is tired of carrying it all.

So, I lay all of it — the hurt, pain, disappointment and fears at the feet of the Beautiful Healer.

Asking Him to touch the raw and bleeding spaces and edges.

To mend them with His healing hands of HOPE and LIFE.

To bring healing to this bleeding heart.

Amen and amen — in the beautiful powerful name of Jesus.

HEAVY DAYS

"I am the Root and the Offspring of David, and the bright Morning Star."

Revelation 22:16

Feet limp and tears fall on a dull

Sunday afternoon in February

Grey fog and showery clouds fit her mood

weariness settles on her being

like a soggy old blanket

She sighs and tries not to think

that the phone didn't ring today

with a voice on the other end

that she longs to hear

No letter arrived in her mailbox

this week, this month

Days weigh heavy with the losses

She wonders about life

as a mother does,

and tries not to lose faith

in a brighter future and

days with more sunshine, laughter

and filled seats at her table

She prays the restlessness will settle

in her "not so fine" being

tonight, as darkness lays long and silent

Does a heart ever forget it's longings?

Can grief subside without a measure of closure?

Will peace override the queasy ache inside her?

She opens her hands, closes her eyes

and releases a tear or two

or three

The whisper is soft

"Daughter, it's ok to let tears fall"

She breathes and lets the sadness

have its moment ... because it's ok

The Father is here

yes, and He is there

He is in the unknown and

the aching longings of a tender heart broken and bleeding

When no one knows, hears, sees

He knows, hears and sees

The Beautiful One knows

The Carrier of bottles of tears

He cares and He sees her

and him

and you

When there are no "answers"

He is the Answer

He is the Heart-Caretaker

He is the Morning Light

after the dark, unsettled and restless

weary evening

He is the beautiful Morning Star

Light-Giver

Hope-Sustainer

Heavenly Healer of broken hearts

She opens wide her heart and arms

in a familiar posture

and in remembrance

She places her hopes in Him

The Morning Star

INTRUDER

"My flesh and my heart may fail, but God is the strength of my heart and my portion forever." Psalm 73:26

Grief — you showed up like the mean bully intruder you are.

Rude.

You barge in and tear my heart to shreds.

You hurl insults, bring up memories that were locked away

and taunt me with my unfulfilled heart-longings.

You flash searingly painful reminders of things I've lost.

That's what you're like and why I try to avoid you.

Lock the door and close the window shades to keep you locked out.

I don't want you here.

You're not invited or wanted.

I don't know why you came, exactly, but I knew you would.

It was inevitable.

Even after all the trying, learning, coping, walking forward, doing all the things

to keep you at bay,

you brazenly waltz in and take a seat at my table.

You slither under the pretty tree lit with soft lights and hung with keepsake ornaments.

Into my peaceful abode you charge

with bold loud ungraceful footsteps.

I don't want you here — no.

If I could punch you in the face, I would!

But I knew you would arrive.

Does it make you happy when my heart rips open, and tears fall unchecked down my cheeks?

When I want to lay my head back down on a soft pillow and dream until well past Christmas?

I'm not sure how to keep walking through December with you.

I try to remember what I know to be true, and I cling to those truths for dear life.

Then I rest my head on His shoulder.

The ever-present, faithful, and kind Abba. Daddy.

He knows all this hard — and He feels all the grief. He isn't scared by my pain and grief.

He patiently, tenderly takes my hand in His strong fatherly one.

He holds me gently and whispers

"Cry if you need to."

And I do.

I do.

The one thing I do know for sure, in it all and through it all

— the ugly grief and pain — is that I'm not alone.

Not abandoned.

Never alone.

My faithful Father — the most Beautiful One — He walks with me.

Immanuel – here with me.

He leads me and sometimes carries me.

Amen

SOMETIMES I CAN BARELY BREATHE

Sometimes I can barely breathe.

My heart races, then skips a beat or two.

I want to scream but swallow instead.

That's how grief feels some days.

And the ache. So much aching.

Like when I remember days long past. Or see an old picture (even though I can barely open a photo album now).

It hurts too much to see the smiling family. Easter dresses and Christmas morning eyes. Summer days bathed in warm sunshine.

Pizza parties, birthday cookie pizzas and loved ones who no longer walk here.

Aching longings that the heart can't speak.

I remember the sound of skateboards clacking, girls giggling, guitars strumming, and the microwave being slammed shut. Laughter and shouting, nagging and dreaming.

Music.

Four wheelers churning tires and tired backpacks leaning against each other on the floor.

I stand at the sink and wash and pray — for clean dishes and clean hearts.

Life passes in a blink or two.

Sometimes I can barely breathe.

I remember — Him — I place the aching and longings and tears in His outstretched palm.

He wants to hold them too.

My Comforter. My Healer.

Beautiful Redeemer.

Redeeming all things, every thing, every aching part.

I let Him. I can give it to Him, knowing He knows the ache too.

And I sit and let Him heal me — lovingly place my tears in a bottle.

Again.

Beautiful Healer.

RAIN YOUR LOVE

Come, Lord Jesus, into our world.

Into this world — all broken and bruised and wildly spinning.

Spinning wildly — our broken worlds.

Shine down your beautiful light into our dark places.

Rain your love into the places where babies fly to heaven

Before they've kissed the earth or seen a mother's smile.

Into the shadows where prodigals stumble and fall.

Fall deep.

Shine your peace where fear causes life to hang in the balance-

hangs wavering.

Cast out shadows that threaten to overwhelm us.

Light equals life.

Come, Lord Jesus.

We long for your beauty and mercy,

long for it to hang like a double rainbow

across two churches that anchor a village.

Heal our wounds.

Bandage our aching.

Hold our hands.

Breathe life into our weary bones, our tired feet.

We wait for you Lord.

Come.

Come, beautiful Lord Jesus.

HOLY BANDAGE

It's been a week Lord — one of those "weeks" that turns into WEEKS.

A week of walking with a hurting heart.

Limping with a painful heart.

Feeling like the knife is twisting, digging deeper into our already aching wound.

How much pain can we endure, keep enduring?

We long for your healing touch, your mercy,

your Holy bandage that will cover the bleeding messiness.

You do see us, Lord?

You see how we are struggling through the week, the day?

We are weak, so weak, leaning on our own strength.

Coming undone — weary.

You DO see us, Lord!

We see you bending down to gently lift us up.

To carry us.

Holding us tight with your nail scarred hands, against your heart which was broken for us.

Your heart that heals us — over and over again.

Heavenly Healer...

It's been a week.

SALTY TEARS

Here's to the tired one who steadily walks on,

the brave one who shows up, shaking and scared.

Here's to the lonely one who aches alone.

So, all alone — the heart broken bleeding one, who smiles through the drippy tears.

Drippy, salty tears. Yes.

You are seen.

Known.

Heard.

Loved.

Seen in the "unseen."

Known in the "unknowing."

Loved in the "unlovely."

The very unlovely, unknowing, unseen place.

Time — it doesn't slow. No.

Pain and grief are "timely" intruders.

In this untimely, unknown place — rest in the arms —

of the timeless, knowing, seeing Father.

Never unseen there.

Aloneness is abandoned, there under His wing.

Grief is gently soothed beside the quiet of His heart — His once broken heart.

He sees the unknown.

He hears the unseen.

And His LOVE is bigger than all the alone — tummy turning loneliness — it's tender,

brave and true.

Real and true LOVE.

Truer than all we know. My God.

Our Father.

Beautiful One.

Seeing.

Knowing.

Hearing.

Loving — it all.

Loving us all.

Adoringly loved.

We thank you — Adored One.

AN UNCLEAR SURRENDERANCE

"...I do believe, help me overcome my unbelief!" Mark 9:24

Lord, help our unbelief.

In the fear, help our unbelief.

When sickness lays our heads low, help our unbelief.

In the unknowing and shadows of unclarity, help our unbelief.

When we walk a twisting road of pain, help our unbelief.

When waves threaten to overwhelm us, again, help our unbelief.

In the valley

on the mountain

in the daily race

in the ordinary, help our unbelief.

In the aching — help our unbelief.

We surrender to your perfect ways

Lord, WE BELIEVE, help our unbelief.

HIS KIND SHOULDER

Come, Lord Jesus, after the storm

when snow lays cold

and gray clouds linger and

when the sun is hidden

here in this place

for now

Come, lift us up

from the place of aching longings

and of hope deferred

Place us on your kind shoulder

and carry us today

when our feet can only limp

not fly

when our hearts weigh us down

like the snowy weight on evergreen limbs

Oh, how we need you Beautiful One

We ask for your peaceful presence

and faithful fatherly kindness

in a seemingly unkind world

where peace is lacking

With open arms and hearts

we surrender the grief and losses

once again

and pray for holy healing bandages

that only You can apply

We LOVE you

we honor you

we adore you

And we desperately need your touch

Beautiful Healer

Beautiful Hope-Giver

Beautiful Abba

Kind Father

Come

WALKING IN CERTAIN UNCERTAINTIES

I'm walking and I ask the Lord to meet me

in this morning of certain uncertainties.

When grief pulls my chest tight.

When dreams lay like puzzle pieces dropped on the floor.

Scattered

Upside down

Missing

When trauma and grief ask a thousand questions

I can't possibly answer.

So, I walk

And talk with my Father.

He knows me and hears me and loves me.

Just the same as yesterday and tomorrow.

Certainly

He is not turned off by my questions and tears.

Quiet tears that slide down on a blue-sky morning walk.

A walk that sounds like mourning doves crying and cardinals singing

and a loud crow squawking.

I close my eyes and breathe and whisper another prayer.

In the unknown uncertainties.

I notice a few red leaves on the trees and the half-moon hanging

in the summer morning sky — like hope.

It reminds me that it is still up there — real — like hope and peace and love.

It still hangs

and the sun still shines

and oxygen still fills my lungs.

Constants

Certainties

Constant certainties I can depend on.

Like heavenly hope

Perfect peace

Lavish love

Unfailing faithfulness

Redemption

My God

Abba...Daddy

I feel His gentle arm around me.

His strong hand holding mine.

His soft shoulder to lean on in the limping.

Constant

Certain

Dependable

That is my Father...

The Beautiful One.

VALLEY OF WALKING AND WAITING

In the valley of walking and waiting

of wrestling and wobbling

when days feel long and the nights longer still

When sleep both eludes and rescues

when feet stumble and hearts limp

— yes even in the limping —

when a thousand thoughts and memories shout and swirl

and shift

When a mid-September day arrives with sadness-tinged beauty

and hope-filled beauty

He is.

He IS

in the sounds of the breeze-blown leaves

In the dancing cotton clouds of a turquoise blue sky

He is

in the whisper of the eagles flying, carried on the wind.

In the shadows laying cool on my river-facing deck

In the sunshine too

And in the still quiet.

His reassuring answer to the restlessness

is the beautiful melody of a text from a friend.

A prayerful loving message from another FB friend.

A grief-focused support group being offered for the hurting (like me).

His message of hope

healing

love

and comfort are

all around me for the taking.

I take

I gratefully receive

And I offer a thousand thanks to my Father for never leaving me alone

My Abba

For always walking with me - into the colorful

shadowy

yet golden

unknown days of Fall.

"Even to your old age and gray hairs I am he, I am he who will sustain

you. I have made you and I will carry you. I will sustain you and I will

rescue you."[1]

WRITING FROM HEARING

The writing came from hearing

the listening came from relationship

the relationship came from surrender

the surrender came from an open heart

and giving up control

The need for control came from trying

to accept something hard

I couldn't change

— which caused distress

and grief and pain

The grief and pain came from loss

hundreds of losses

Slowly, over time

the grief and pain

turned into reluctant acceptance

acceptance turned into giving up

the need for control

This turned into arms wide

and heart-wide-open surrender

and this turned into beautiful relationship

where I could hear His voice

Which turned into a miracle

of writing my story

which is really His story

Amen

SOMEBODY'S SON

I wonder as I walk

why is this my story?

how is this our story?

I wonder

I saw him as I walked toward

the grocery store

He played a melody on a drum

standing in the freezing sunshine

on a bitter February morning

alone

And I thought to myself

I'll give him some money on my way out

yes, on my way out

praying I wouldn't forget

We all passed him by

busy mothers, gray haired grandmas

rushing truck drivers

all of us busy with our busy lives

I wondered, did any of us notice?

On my way out I started reaching

for my wallet and the cash

I'd been saving

for the perfect opportunity to use it

in this debit-cashless-tap and go-world

I KNEW this was the moment

and I gently laid the money

in his navy knitted hat

He now sat on the icy cold snow

maybe he was tired

of being tired

In that moment my eyes met his

and I memorized his face

words formed on my lips

but didn't escape my mouth

I turned to go with a small wave

— not enough!

oh, not nearly enough I thought

and I turned

and locked eyes with him again

until tears started leaking out of my eyes and down my frozen
cheeks

A voice in my head screamed,

he's somebody's brother

uncle

father

friend

grandson

son

He is somebody's son

sitting alone

beating a melody on a drum

alone

On my walk I wonder

what is his story?

why is my story mine?

Maybe so I can see things

more clearly

differently

than I ever did before

through a heavenly lens

I hear my Abba

the Beautiful One whisper

it's ok to let tears leak out of your eyes

it's ok to be human

it's ok

And I breathe a prayer

in the freezing February sunshine

for somebody's son.

SLIPPERY SLOPE

"...the Lord makes firm the steps of the one who delights in him." Psalm 37:23

All morning she listens to the

argument in her head of wanting to go

but knowing the roads are icy

treacherous and uninviting

Her heart wants to go

but her mind says stay

After lunch, her boots are laced

and her mitts are tucked in

and she walks head down

watching the road

guiding her feet and also

stealing upward glances of the sun

It peeks at her and

warms her nose and

kisses her cheeks

The road is slippery and ice-packed

slushy and wet

it's uneven and bent

It slopes upward and around a bend

turning this way and that

She hears her own crunchy footsteps

and nature's music

alive with chickadee songs

When she turns at the stop sign

the sun sits at her back

but the wind whips her scarf

'round her chin

At the dip in the road

her eyes scan the distance

for oncoming cars

and watch her steps for bare road

Once

Twice — her foot slips

and she reaches for air

Her hood is up and down

her mitts are on and then off

The journey

ever changing

ever moving

ever evolving — 'til she's home

and her boots retrace

her snowy footsteps

back to her house and warmth

She looks at the driveway

a sheet of hard silver ice

a slippery slope

one might say

to be avoided at all costs

She thinks to herself that this walk

and her own journey

aren't so different

after all

— she remembers —

Keep your eyes up

listen for the music

keep watching the sun

and the Son

Keep your feet on the path

keep on walking

and avoid the slippery slopes.

HELP — I REFUSE

"My flesh and my heart may fail, but God is the strength of my heart and my

portion forever." Psalm 73:26

"Go see a counselor," they said.

"Get some help," they suggested.

...a shrink?

I didn't want to.

Oh, I knew she was nice enough.

Smart enough. She came highly recommended.

But I still rebelled against it — the idea.

A counselor?

She doesn't know me; I don't know her. How could she possibly understand the situation —

let alone help?

I sat in the chair across from her. She smiled.

We talked about "the situation." When I left, I thought, *Well, that was fine, but I don't think*

it helped.

I didn't feel different. At all.

After a couple more sessions I called it quits.

Hurt, bleeding, wrecked, I called again.

Another appointment sitting across from her in a gray chair. Then another. And another.

Weeks, months of sessions.

To be honest — I still sit across from her — and hubby too.

And there's been healing. And bandages and hope placed across gaping wounds.

Boundaries set. Thinking reframed.

It's not magic.

Sometimes it's downright ugly. But it works.

I'm a Christian. God is my ultimate "heart-garden caretaker."

Yes.

I'd be lost without Him and His goodness and mercies new every morning.

My portion. Manna.

"Stay with it," they say.

My counselor, she gives me tools and teaches me healthy ways to process and think about my trauma, grief, and shame.

I don't pretend to be a doctor who knows how to treat

physical ailments or diseases so how could I possibly know exactly
how to heal my own

emotional issues and broken heart?

Thank you, Father — for beautiful godly counselors and the healing
tools they impart to us.

Thank you, Father — for HOPE and healing and JOY in the middle
of the fire. For walking me

through it all and helping me see my need for wise healthy counsel.

Unwavering in kindness and astounding in faithfulness, that is my
God.

PAIN SAYS

Pain says, "I can't do this."

He says, "You can do all things with my help."

Grief cries, "I'm broken and scared."

He says, "I am the beautiful Comforter, and you are never alone."

Trauma shouts, "I don't know where to turn for help."

He says, "Cast all your cares and anxiety on me, the great Physician."

The Liar sneers, "You are beyond help, lost and hopeless."

He says, "I am the way the truth and the life. Follow me."

In all of life's hard things He is the soft, kind and gentle voice,

speaking TRUTH over our achingly broken lives.

Speak Father,

I'm listening.

Abba.

ROADS UNNAVIGABLE

"Yet I will rejoice in the Lord, I will be joyful in God my Savior."
Habakkuk 3:18

On a September day, 35 years ago, my world got turned upside down.

At nineteen years old, I became a first-time mom and a widow on the same day. My young husband died in a car accident on the way to the hospital where I had given birth. My dad unknowingly came upon the accident scene and then had to break the news to me—his youngest daughter.

Thankfully, I was a believer, and God carried me through this tragedy and trial with His gentle kindness. He covered me in a blanket of love and sustained me with His peace, unexplainable peace.

In the following weeks and months, I cared for my baby son, and my life got rearranged as God directed my path. The next year I married my husband Alex, and he adopted my son, and we grew our family by adding two daughters.

Fast forward 34 years and I have faced many more trials, and many joys too of course. Joys like birthdays, grand babies, weddings, family reunions, and sitting under the warm summer sun with my feet in the sand.

Job losses, sickness, death of my parents, children moving away, and "empty nest" have also marked my journey.

A grown child I love walks a rocky road of addiction, crisis, incarceration, and pain; therefore, I feel the weight and angst of this situation. It's a path I never thought we would walk as a family. The road is mostly unnavigable, grief-ridden, and scary.

Through it all God leads and weaves His peace, hope, and kindness along my path.

I choose to keep hoping in Him, walking with my hand in His and leaning on His strong, kind shoulder.

Writer is a new name I've been given this year.

I've started writing His words, words He has given me, as an act of obedience. I'm being vulnerable and telling my story, which is really His story.

Grace, hope, healing and love inked on a page.

I will keep writing and lifting Him up, thankful for His kind faithfulness to me.

His praise is always on my lips.

MOM

Sometimes on the breath of a warm summer evening's breeze, I hear her voice.

I see her smile.

And the ache settles again in my chest.

It's there, but I'm not sad.

Not too sad.

She loved the songs of chickadees

and sparrows.

She fed them in a wooden feeder on her front lawn.

She hated it when the blue jays acted like bullies.

Their songs sing her name in the gentle quiet evening.

The sun is slowly sinking but still warm.

A fire crackles and snaps as my husband stirs it to flames.

The soft breeze gently lifts my hair, and I smile.

I remember her face.

And her voice — like a melody.

She loved it when we had a bonfire. She could let down her hair, so to speak, and enjoy a roasted marshmallow or two. Maybe even a hot dog!

I imagine it reminded her of her own childhood days.

Later, she and my dad would meander down Cobblestone drive in a white Ford Tempo.

The summer moon and a thousand stars twinkling down on them.

They'd wave and smile.

My children would wave and call out, "Goodbye, Nan."

The car brake lights would blink as they slowly edged down the long lane.

Then they'd disappear, over the last hill.

I miss those days and cherish the sweet memories that muse in my head on a June evening.

I'll see you later, mom.

The Next Day, a Funeral

"So do not fear, for I am with you, do not be dismayed, for I am your God, I will strengthen you and help you, I will uphold you with my righteous right hand!" Isaiah 41:10

I don't remember if the words were actually audible or not. Barely nineteen and a widow with a newborn son, sitting in the back seat of my father's car, waiting for a ferry to take us to our island home. But the words spoken were as clear as if they were.

Unquestionable. Undeniable. Real.

Words spoken over me by my Heavenly Father, of peace and hope for a future.

"Don't fear, my daughter."

The words were not a whisper too quiet to hear; they were a strong declaration. "PEACE" spoken in the grief. I don't remember what I was wearing, or if my three-day-old baby boy was awake or sleeping, or what color car my dad drove.

The journey from the hospital to home—a blur. But the words He spoke over my shattered dreams and broken heart—peace and hope—clear, yet unexplainable.

You know, the PEACE that passes understanding—yes, that peace.

Friends, family, and acquaintances dropped by with cards, gifts, casseroles, and heartfelt condolences. Chocolate cake and crocheted blankets, hugs and tears, too.

The next day a funeral with a sturdy oak casket laying across the front of a little church. I don't remember much of that either—not the scriptures read nor the songs sung. No.

But I do recall how I felt—PEACE, hope, and love from my Father.

Confidence in His care. Held. Not forgotten.

On funeral day, clouds emptied rain, gloomy and dreary. Standing at my mom's kitchen window after the service I noticed a rainbow—no wait—a double rainbow. It stretched from one end of my tiny fishing village to the other.

A sign? Yes...a sign.

Hope, peace, love, life, confidence, and joy (yes, even JOY) written in the muted colors of a double rainbow—stretching wide with a message. I didn't doubt it, or even question it.

I smiled and believed it. I still do.

Fighting My Battles

"...His praise will always be on my lips." Psalm 34:1

The kitchen window called to me. I should have been packing up boxes, dreams, memories, but I started to sing. I can't remember the song, but it was a worship song I knew, and I was belting it out.

It was what I knew to do, and it helped with the pain. You see, only a few weeks before, I had buried my husband—and a box-full of dreams, too. My tiny baby boy slept in a nursery at my mom's house, in my childhood bedroom. Instead of rocking my baby in our house, dreaming, and planning for the future, I was packing up plates, cups, and sheets.

I didn't know where God was leading me, or what the next month, or year held, but I DID KNOW He held me. He had spoken love, peace, and hope to my broken heart, days after my husband died in a car accident on the very day our son was born.

So, I sang, arms open wide, giving it all to the Healer of my heart. He heard me; I know it. I didn't realize at the time (or maybe I did) that worship was how I "fought my battles"—against grief and loss and uncertainty. He met me in the "sacrifice of praise" and lifted me up, as

I lifted up His name.

Looking back now at that young woman, packing up shattered dreams into boxes, turning the corner into a new life, I'd like to say "Hey, the road ahead looks much easier, wider, safer, more comfortable."

But no, that wouldn't be the whole truth. Yes, many blessings and happy days—a loving husband who adopted our son and two beautiful daughters to complete our family.

Yet, the next 30 years or so have had their share of curve balls, crises, uncertainties, and grief. That is life...

Change is constant.

And, also constant is His love, mercy, and grace. He is my hope, peace and joy—who I cling to daily.

My Portion, my Manna.

His faithfulness, kindness, and goodness have followed me every step I've taken.

Still today, if you were to peek into my kitchen, you would see me standing on tiptoes, arms up, fighting my battles.

SOMETIMES, SOMEHOW

"Now faith is confidence in what we hope for and assurance about what we do not see."

Hebrews 11:1

Even grown, they are still my "kids."

I still call them kids, and oh, how I love them.

The ones I nurtured —

taught to walk, talk, ride a bike

and be polite.

All the things.

Of course, hubby helped, too.

My daughters post beautiful "grown up" pictures of themselves on IG and FB, and I see

three-year-olds with pigtails and knobby knees.

Gap-tooth grins and chocolate chip cookie monsters. Pizza devourers.

You hear me — am I right?

You get it.

Our children are gifts; masterpieces created by the artistic, loving Creator.

All thanks and glory go to Him.

I will always be their "mom,"

and they will always live in my heart.

In the deepest part of my being — treasured,

held close, loved.

But sometimes, somehow, life gets "messy."

Turned upside down and wrecked a little

or a lot. Ouch.

How?

Why?

When?

I don't know.

It feels like the painting got all messed up, crazy, kind of ugly.

Downright ugly in fact at times.

A child I love loses their way — a wayward prodigal.

The beautiful colors and music I once knew get distorted

crazily mixed,

and I can't see the whole picture anymore.

Just "gray tones"

and "off tune" melodies.

It's hard to see the original piece.

Especially through tears and trauma.

Yes, and the aching pain, a ripped apart heart.

I've thought about it a lot — the masterpiece.

Is it still there?

Underneath the wreckage?

Hidden by the consequences of unhealthy living and twisted choices?

I've listened for the truth.

Prayed, and yes, cried for it.

Longed for an answer, for wholeness,

beauty and life

— for him

for me

for us.

The Beautiful One says,

"Yes, believe in hope and new life.

"Redemption," the Redeemer softly whispers.

How?

Why?

When?

I don't know.

But I believe — in the HOPE that He gives — every day.

Hope that says one day there will be sounds of music

and a colorful mosaic of beauty again.

Vibrant colors that speak life,

wholeness,

rebirth.

Guitar melodies strumming HOPE.

Songs with a thousand harmonies.

Dancing and colors and grace.

Somehow.

Somewhere.

Someday.

I keep believing.

HOPE

"May the God of hope fill you with all joy and peace as you trust in him, so that you may overflow with hope by the power of the Holy Spirit."
Romans 15:13

A word written in chalk on my chalkboard a couple of springs ago. It was my word for the year.

I needed it — badly.

So, I wrote it out and looked at it daily.

I wasn't really sure about the word, but I *hoped* and *prayed* for HOPE.

It had been a difficult year, trying to process pain and grief. Those emotions weren't new for me, but they still felt so raw.

My heart bled.

I was limping through what felt like a long "winter" into a season of spring.

The colors were muted, the sun a bit shaded, and I was tired.

So tired.

Walking in the valley I realized that hope is a fragile thing. It can easily get lost behind the rubbish of broken dreams and broken hearts.

So very fragile and slippery, seeping through our fingers while we try to hang onto it.

"When hope is crushed, the heart is crushed..."[13]

SIGH.

But I began to see that hope isn't a thing, something I can "find," it's Someone.

Hope's name is Jesus.

Hope of the world. YES!

So, I began to cling to Him, instead of looking around me for an elusive feeling.

He is real, and ALIVE and He radiates HOPE.

I sat in the sunshine of His hope.

Oh, the beautiful hope of His death and resurrection.

Hope awakened, restored and renewed.

In clinging (and I do mean clinging) to this hope,

I saw the beauty around.

I felt the beauty of hope, not in my circumstance (that hadn't changed) but in Jesus' presence.

In His goodness, kindness and faithfulness.

In speaking hope to others, I was also speaking hope to myself.

Remembering.

Reminding myself.

I have a living hope — Jesus Christ.

HER FRIEND STOPPED BY

Her friend stopped by with a Christmas gift. Sweet.

They chatted over coffee, and she opened it — a book.

The Broken Way by one of her favorite authors, Ann Voskamp.

It was a nice enough book. It looked fine.

A good read she knew.

But here's the thing, did she dare open it? Let her eyes rest on the words, maybe words

that would be too hard to accept?

Broken.

She knew all about it and wished she didn't.

Did she want to read about it — she wasn't sure. I mean, being broken was one thing, trying to read about it was another thing. Hard.

She smiled, thanked her beautiful friend, and laid the book aside.

For another day. Another month or even year.

But it beckoned. Daring her to read the words — maybe there was treasure inside the covers?

Indeed, there was! HEALING that seeps in gently through wounds.

Voskamp writes "...there is no growth without change, no change without surrender, no surrender without wound — no abundance without breaking. Wounds are what break open the soul to plant the seeds of a deeper growth."[14] Ouch — but YES!

She knew it as she read the pages over the next few weeks. Saw the truths revealed line by line.

Beauty from ashes. Beauty from being broken and healed. Communion in the sacred woundedness.

"Maybe the love gets in easier right where the heart's broke open," Voskamp writes.[15]

YES. YES. YES.

An agreeing, and with that came peace.

Hope for another day of the journey knowing she walks hand in hand

with the healer – Jehovah-Rapha.

She picks the book up again, reminding herself of the beauty in the broken way.

His way. The beautifully broken way.

The ONLY way.

She turns the page and reads on.

RAINY FUNERAL

"For I know the plans I have for you, declares the Lord, plans to prosper you and not to harm you, plans to give you HOPE and a future." Jeremiah 29:11

The doctors told my mom I wouldn't live.

Grand Mal seizures. Bleeding from the brain. Sick unto death.

"Buy her a funeral dress," they said. I've been told this story all my life.

I'm sure it was a scary time for my parents — a baby girl born many years

after the family was complete.

And to hear this news — sad, heartbreaking.

They say it was a "miracle" because well, here I am. Alive and well.

The doctors couldn't explain it. There was no funeral that week, only rejoicing in a life given.

It's a neat story to hear and sometimes wonder about. I never really knew a lot of details.

Only the main parts — important ones. And that is enough to see that God had a purpose.

Has a purpose (for this life) and yours.

My life has been marked by a tragedy or two, ups and downs, an uneven and rocky path.

But also, by beauty and mercy and grace. Amazing grace!

Double rainbows on a rainy, funeral day.

Unexplainable peace in unspeakable grief.

Strength that says it won't let go.

Blessings too many to count (even though I'm writing them in my journal).

Beautiful people who call me wife, mom, Nana, sister, and friend.

Lavish love and breathtaking beauty surround my life.

So even though I walk an uneven, ragged path that sometimes overwhelms, PEACE and LOVE walk with me — His eyes are always on me.

I've seen the evidence — clearly.

That's why I speak. The message is bigger, so much bigger and more beautiful

than my story.

It's His story — retold.

You see I'm just a little girl from a little fishing village on a little island,

who loves and serves a BIG God.

A *right mighty big God.*

A PRAYER NOT YET ANSWERED

Finding hope in the darkness, in the pain of watching a loved one

Struggling in crisis and wandering.

In the valley that seems too long, and impossibly difficult.

Finding hope in the valley, in the heavenly quiet

sitting in the middle of unanswered prayers

I don't even...

I don't even know.

I don't even know how.

And yet,

and yet I do.

I do know how.

And I do know.

And somehow, I do.

Oh, trust me when I say it isn't easy.

So not easy.

Like searching for glimpses of sunshine on the cloudiest day.

Like walking in sucking dirty mud, or finding the energy

to take full complete breaths.

Ones that fully fill the lungs — that fill all the needy organs with life-giving oxygen.

Yes, kind of like that.

Doable.

Attainable.

Possible.

Also draining, heavy, and seemingly unreachable.

I ask how?

I ask why?

Is it even real?

And if so, what path brought me to this place?

This unknowing, almost unnavigable place?

This I-don't-want-to-be-here-or-walk-here place.

Really, there's no one to ask.

No one with answers, I think.

Well, who am I kidding...my counselor has answers, of course.

And a map of seemingly unnavigable places and roads —

harsh, rocky, cold roads — where no one wants to walk.

A busy, but lonely road.

Looking for beauty and hope

one eye open, and one eye closed in prayer.

Please God...

Searching for peace, and a quiet river to rest beside.

And meaning for the pain.

It's the endless walking it out, looking behind, glancing ahead

and trying to stay in the right lane.

Without being bulldozed or side-lined. *sigh *

I know you hear me, friend.

Your heart sighs a little in knowing someone else feels the hurt,

confusion, and fear.

The fear that crawls inside your belly and bed some nights.

Different roads and traffic signs, but the same tired, limping feet,
and shaky smile.

Friend you aren't alone — we aren't alone.

And so, like most journeys, the road is navigated one step, day

or moment at a time.

It can't be more

Or less — in order to keep moving ahead in hope.

Yes, HOPE.

Always hope!

My faithful Father steadies the weak and fragile heart with His hope.

With His tender love.

And a strong faithful shoulder to lean on

in the limp-walking.

Hopeful-walking.

My daily Portion.

Manna.

Always just enough of what I need

for each day I find in Him.

Strength for my body,

hope for my spirit,

enduring peace for my soul.

My God.

ELIJAH, MY FRIEND

"...the angel of the Lord came back a second time and touched him and said, "Get up and eat, for the journey is too much for you." 1 Kings 19:7

Elijah and I have become good friends this year. During a six-week study on him with some friends, his story was brought to life in a new way for me. I loved it. I think what made me love the study, and Elijah, too, was seeing his humanity. (Of course, I knew he was human—not news.) But I learned about his *humanness*—how he was weak, tired, and scared...just like me.

Oh, he had his moment of FIRE where he literally "stood strong" on the mountain. He showed bravery, grit, and unwavering trust in his faithful, powerful God. Abba. Jehovah-Jireh. Provider and Sustainer. He didn't back down to the earthly powers that tried to muscle him to defeat. *No!*

He proclaimed God's judgment on Israel and the land. He stood on the words of His Father and called down Holy Fire to defeat the prophets of Baal. *Wow!* He also trusted God with his very life—for food, for shelter and for sustenance.

Elijah inspires me to be braver, bolder, and stronger!

On the flip side, I've also seen him in his weaker moments. Like when he fled in fear from Queen Jezebel—literally ran for his life! Alone and trembling, he hid in caves. Here he didn't feel so brave or strong or bold. Nope. He was living in a different season, a difficult valley that tested his human frailties. Ohhhh, that I get. I understand that season too well. (More than I'd like to if I'm being honest.)

Honest, hard, gritty "life stuff." Yes.

But when I read 1 Kings 19:7, I sighed a sigh of relief. I think Elijah and I could be good friends—we'd really get each other. He, the strong bold prophet, and me, the common girl from a tiny fishing village. Friends.

Different life experiences, same Father.

Elijah, worn down by his trial and fears, laid down under a bush. And God provided food for him because "the journey is too much for you."

Ahhhhh, I understand that too. I'm betting you do, too, friend.

The journey is too much for you, for me. Yes, it is.

But for God?

God in His beautiful kindness and faithfulness, feeds me my daily portion. He gives me what I need to survive the day.

I don't need to beg for it, or work for it.

He knows—He KNOWS.

He gently hands me what I need—strength, peace, hope, joy—while gazing at me with eyes soft with love. His astounding, amazing, and kind LOVE.

I KNOW I'm thankful, like Elijah.

ELEPHANT SITS ON MY CHEST

"You make your saving help my shield, and your right hand sustains me, your help has made me great. You provide a broad path for my feet.... The Lord lives! Praise be to my Rock! Exalted be God my Savior!" Psalm 18:35-36,46.

I'm driving my car to work, and an elephant sits on my chest.

Dark. Mean. Brooding.

Grief

I wonder why...still?

I mean, I've done the work, haven't I?

Talked to the counselor, read the books, cried, and screamed.

Ran my heart out. *sigh *

Yet the elephant sits — unmoving.

I could ask politely for him to leave but he's quite comfortable. I want to tell him that he's hindering the sunlight, the air I breathe, my eyesight.

That he slows my walking — like in a fog.

My thoughts move to the fog along the beach—ah, a place I love.

Fond memories of the seashore. Days that stretch before me, sand in my toes,

salt air lifting my hair, the sun on my face.

No elephants.

In my mind I walk along the water's edge, the sand swirling around my feet.

Saltiness in the breeze, on my tongue, mixing with my tears.

Isn't salt healing? I ask myself.

"Yes," He whispers. "Let them flow."

As I walk, He takes my hand (in my remembering) and leads me.

"I'm walking with you, daughter, and when you stumble, I'll carry you."

Like that poem, you know the one. "Footprints."

Yes.

Being carried. Lightness.

Unhindered.

Like a trusting child, that's me.

Unafraid of the grief because He's not afraid of it either, and He walks with me.

You see grief isn't His story or THE story or my story.

My story is still being written, not in sand, but on a strong foundation.

The sun sets, my hand in His,

and I quietly rest.

BELIEVING

"Then Jesus told him, 'Because you have seen me, you have believed. Blessed are those who have not seen and yet have believed.'" John 20:29

Maybe the answer doesn't come...today.

Or tomorrow.

Or next year.

Maybe the healing is a lifetime removed from us.

Maybe we limp — while praying and hoping and even believing.

Praying for the "believing hoping."

Praying and hoping for the believing.

You see, we can hope and not "see" the hoped for.

Oh, and we can believe for the not seen "hoped for."

See?

He is in it all — the Hoping.

Believing.

Praying.

He IS: hope, belief, and the whispered prayer.

In the unknowing, I can believe for the unseen, and I can hope.

Even in the unknown.

And in the seemingly hopelessness,

and unknowing, and unbelief,

I trust.

I trust Him.

I choose to trust Him.

I trust that HE IS GOOD.

He is God.

He is the GOOD God.

God of the unknown, unseen

and undone.

I believe...even in the unseeing.

BE BRAVE

"So do not fear for I am with you, do not be afraid for I am your God. I will strengthen you and help you, I will uphold you with my righteous right hand." Isaiah 41:10

A pretty journal adorns my nightstand.

I love the way it looks sitting there, all peaceful, with swirly gold lettering. And I love the message on the cover—be brave.

Yes. Brave!

I want to be brave—I truly do.

I see bravery in the people in my life: my daughters, husband, family, and friends.

In my Bible, friends like Queen Esther, Father Abraham, and bold Elijah meet me, too. But it seems almost impossible to walk in their shoes.

It's so easy to see bravery in them, in others, am I right?

Putting on a brave face has been mine to do a few times in my life, like when I became a widow and a new mom, (on the same day), at nineteen-years-old.

When I said yes to my new husband and turned the corner into a new life, I was also practicing bravery. When I moved away from my island community to the mainland with my little family—brave. Oh, and when I put on my "big girl clothes" and flew out west, alone, to visit my daughter and her family—very brave.

Sometimes you just do the brave thing without even thinking about it too much, perhaps it's easier if your bravery will benefit another?

Other times being brave feels just too hard. Too much.

Overwhelming.

Bravery can look like speaking hope and beauty from the trenches of grief and trauma. Like writing letters of hope to a loved one in prison. Praying for healing, restoration and "new life."

Recently I've felt God nudging me to write. To write my story—share the beauty in the broken, the message in the mess.

His story told through mine.

Singing has always been easier for me, but writing, it feels awkward at times and a bit stilted.

But God, He pushes my pen.

Because He wouldn't give up on the message...or the girl. The Messenger has a beautiful story of grace, peace, hope and faithfulness—even in the trenches. Especially in the trenches.

So, I write my story which is really His story.

His story of mercy and grace, peace, healing, and hope.

The Beautiful Healer, He walks with me and holds my hand, the tiny, calloused hand of the common island girl.

Leaning on Him, I rest and walk on in the light of His beauty.

I can be brave, leaning on His strong arms of HOPE.

NO NEWS IS...

Four weeks and no word from her son. Twenty-eight days.

And she IS counting.

The night's darkness sometimes brings fear,

it slips into bed beside her.

FEAR.

It squeezes her heart, again. A familiar yet uninvited guest.

She whispers a prayer and hopes for tomorrow.

Maybe she will get a call then, after work.

Maybe.

She tries not to think about the next "holiday."

Easter — so much to rejoice about and in. Her Savior's life-giving
death

and His beautiful awakening resurrection.

Amazing!! THE GREATEST STORY.

But also...family gatherings and egg hunts and ham dinners.

And empty seats.

It is easier, most of the time...some of the time.

But the ache.

It lingers in the hallways and laughter.

It floats on the spring breeze.

Still.

Then she remembers that His HOPE is also seated here — in this place.

LOVE sits in the empty seat and whispers "Do not fear daughter."

And PEACE spreads a warm sunshine blanket over the skies.

Over her heart.

In the ache — He walks beside her.

Still.

Always.

FACILIMENTE

(sing with ease and without strain)

CAN YOU HEAR HIM?

Can you hear Him speaking today?

His voice like a soft, sweet melody?

It whispers a love song above the loud voices of

doubt

and fear

and shameful lies.

Over clinging grief.

It falls on my ears like the soft sound of red

maple leaves falling from my front yard tree.

Resting on a carpet of still green lawn.

Almost imperceptible.

Yet, noticed.

Oh, it's not easy to hear sometimes on the noisy

rocky walk of life — His voice. It can get silenced

by shouts and lies — and blinding dark.

Sneering dark.

Yes, the darkest valley can hide His voice at times.

But oh, don't forget, His kind voice is there.

I won't forget — it is there

and here.

Right here today.

Like the gentle rustling of the golden leaves

falling sideways across the road.

Like the melody of an old hymn that reminds me

"It is well with my soul."

Like the warm gentle hand of a kind father

rocking his baby to sleep.

Peaceful.

Quiet.

Strong but gentle.

Soothing like a lullaby.

I'm listening for His voice of peace today.

Abba, speak.

I'm looking for Him.

I'm waiting, arms open, for Him.

I want to see Him — His tender kind eyes offering

all the love a father can give a child.

Like me.

Like you.

With childlike faith I wait and listen and watch.

I turn my head and hope to catch a glimpse of His hand.

Even though my eyes can't see Him, the eyes of

my heart sees Him clearly.

A clear "knowing" of hearts that are known.

Seen and known.

Without a doubt I know He sits beside me

while I soak up rays in my peach deck chair

watching bees drink nectar

from a yellow mum plant.

His voice of peace surrounds me

and I rest in His watchful care.

Can you hear Him speaking today?

His voice speaks like a soft, sweet melody.

Amen.

ORDER

Order makes me happy.

I like it when things have a place, a sequence, an appointed time or space. Yes.

My old photo albums are ordered by dates and time of events.

My daily routine is ordered to flow in an easily navigated path—usually—like that, too.

Disruptions sometimes turn me around and leave me feeling upside down.

Small disruptions don't bother me too much, but bigger harder ones leave me limping a bit-

or a lot.

I think we are all like that, maybe.

God ordered the stars and planets, also the days, months and years.

He IS order.

Everything He has created or planned has order to it.

I really love that.

It gives me peace in knowing my Father is a God of order.

He understands my flailing when things are not going as I hoped or dreamed.

When I'm living in a space of disorder because of this earthly life's challenges and chaos,

I can rest in His peace, His beautiful order.

Peaceful order—ordered by Him.

Only in His arms—I find peace and rest.

Order.

A SECRET GIFT

"I remain confident of this: I will see the goodness of the Lord in the land of the living."

Psalms 27:13

It was a gift from my "secret pal."

Remember that thing we used to do? Give gifts to our fellow sisters in secret.

Fun, I loved doing it. I received a little African violet in a cute, little, plant pot

from my "sister," Sally.

Sweet.

I carefully brought it home and set it in a spot I thought would be just perfect. To be honest I didn't know much about African violets. I didn't know they were beautiful, but they were a bit finicky. My mom said, "Oh, it'll die. I could never keep one alive."

Great, I thought to myself.

My mom had a green thumb.

She had nurtured spider plants, ivies, many other plants, and they thrived under her care.

Me, not so much. I'd only had a couple of plants and wasn't sure I would know how

to keep this pretty plant alive.

I wanted to.

I hoped I could.

Well, maybe my little plant heard my mom talking. Maybe it just had a lot of grit,

or maybe I DO have a green thumb because it's thriving 27 years later!

I know, right?! It's been divided and repotted and gifted more times than I can count.

This makes me smile so big.

Right now, though, it isn't blooming.

I really don't know why. Nothing has changed that I know of.

I'm tending it with all the tender love and gentle care I always have.

I'm trying to be patient. Truly. I'm trying to not worry.

Is it sick? Is it too dry or wet, too hot, or cold?

I don't remember it ever going this long without blooming.

I really want to see some pretty flowers. My friend posts pictures of her plant

with gorgeous purple flowers.

I even talk to it sometimes. Nothing.

It sits...waiting.

Like me.

Even though it seems long in the waiting, I know one morning I will awake

to tiny violet blooms. I know it.

I know it!

I have HOPE for blooms.

And new beginnings.

New life.

Newfound freedom.

Restoration.

Dancing.

Because where there is hope in Him there is LIFE.

YES!

He brings dead things to life.

Jesus restores, heals, binds up, carries.

He redeems our broken and weary stories.

He makes tired plants, and people, bloom.

Beautifully.

HOPE.

THE TASTE OF BITTERNESS

"How long must I wrestle with my thoughts and day after day have sorrow in my heart?...But I trust in your unfailing love; my heart rejoices in your salvation. I will sing the Lord's praise, for He has been good to me." Psalms 13:2,5,6

Anger isn't usually my song.

Bitterness isn't what my tongue speaks.

Discouragement and despair aren't my heart's message.

Cuss words aren't my language of choice.

Lament, however, is a heart cry I often sing.

By Webster's definition a lament is "a crying out in grief."

A cry of heart break that reaches *to* and *for* the heavens.

In a Biblical sense, a lament is a form of prayer. A prayer that acknowledges and expresses sorrow, pain, injustice, and then turns to hope and trust—that God hears me and sees me and is walking me through the fire.

My counselor says it's normal and ok to lament—even healthy.

A lament isn't without hope; it doesn't ultimately point to despair.

She also said that the Bible is full of lament.

Interesting, I think to myself. Over a third of the psalms are a lament— a questioning, a crying out, a longing, and then a choosing to trust God. Lamentations is a whole book devoted to this "crying out to God." Job cried out to God and waited on Him in his suffering. Even Jesus lamented in the garden of Gethsemane.

It's normal that I feel sad and heavy-hearted about broken, painfully hard situations in my life. It's also okay to question God, He can handle it. He's not afraid of my questions, and He's always there to listen. I'm thankful for that.

Here's what I need to know and remember: sorrow and joy can co-exist.

I can feel sorrow and also joy. I'm so thankful for that.

Feeling sorrow in a moment doesn't mean I have to walk in it all day or even all week. I can wake up feeling joy tomorrow—and the next day, too. I can smile, laugh, and enjoy the day.

I can hug my family, take a walk, sing, and dance and praise!

God is in both: the lament and the singing. He is with me in both joy and sorrow. That truth makes me smile so big.

Sometimes I forget this truth, or it gets hidden under the weight of pain and sorrow. So, I do what I need to do to remember—I write the truths down. Using my favorite pink pens, I write down Bible verses that declare truth and I set them on my windowsill. When I'm washing dishes, I can read them every day.

I stick them on my fridge, and I say them out loud. On repeat.

I sing them in the car and on my walks.

Because this girl needs to be reminded some days that God is walking with me and is giving me strength for each new day.

Strength for the hard day and for the easier one, too.

"But the Lord stood at my side and gave me strength..."[16]

A small white card with this verse written on it sat on my windowsill for several months and became my daily hope. Then one day I mailed it off in an envelope to someone I dearly love and who I thought may need to be reminded of this truth too.

I love this verse because it speaks and prophesies truth and hope over my life.

I claim it.

It was true for the Apostle Paul, and it's true for me.

Even on the days when I don't FEEL strong, He stands with me holding me up. He is so kind and so good.

On the days when I feel like praise-dancing, I do.

Arms up, hands open, feet twirling.

On the other days when my feet feel like lead stones and

my heart aches, I sing a prayer of lament.

A heart song that whispers an intimate cry for help and feels peace in knowing He hears me.

A beautiful heart connection between my Father and me—where I am known and heard.

I'm heard, known, and deeply loved.

I don't beat myself up either because I know—I KNOW—God wants both of my songs. They are both equally beautiful to Him because they both reach from my heart to His—a melodious love song. And with His merciful love song He reaches down to me—an ordinary wife, momma and Nana, and answers my cry.

Again and again.

He is faithful.

GRAY DAYS

Beautiful One

we long for your BEAUTY

on these gray days of bitter cold

When our hearts almost stop beating

at times

When our tired feet stumble

on the wintry path

When our eyes droop from

sunless mornings

And when we don't know how

to whisper prayerful words

or how to preach hopeful words to ourselves

Help us to sing your hope over our hurts

Cover us with your wings of

PEACE in the pain

and grant us GRACE in the grief

Lord, we believe- help our unbelief

Show us the beauty of the Son

when we lack the warmth of the sun

and its golden beauty is hidden

Your beauty is our HOPE

Grasp our fragile hands and lead us

to hope-filled meadows of LIFE

Our hearts adore you

our lips sing your praises

and we wait for you

Beautiful One

We long to see YOUR beauty

in these gray days

of bitter cold

SPINNING

My morning drive to work begins with a prayer.

Whispered prayers for family and friends who are struggling.

Whispers turn into words, words become wobbly, and tears follow.

Quiet, silent tears.

In a world that feels tilted, spinning too fast, and yet tired.

So tired.

I've said it before while driving, or walking in the quiet, "Come, Lord Jesus."

Come, we're holding onto hope by a thread.

My daughter echoed the same prayer yesterday...

"Come, Lord Jesus."

Yes.

Our hearts long for His coming,

His kingdom,

His peaceful presence in our whirlwind worlds.

Twirling and spinning,

dizzy

and sometimes downright scary.

Lonely, too...

An isolating, quarantining, and lonely world.

Irregular.

And a sadness that speaks no words.

The morning sun lays on the misty river as I drive by.

Beauty in the messiness.

Morning misty-river beauty seen through misty eyes.

Another whispered prayer

Come Lord Jesus...come

He does

He will

He is HERE.

Right in the middle of our twirling irregular, sometimes sad days...

Lives

Worlds.

I grasp His hand tight, and He holds mine, gently and warmly.

Firmly loving

Like a father would.

His peace settles like mist on a gray river morning.

He is here — Hallelujah

The Beautiful Hand Holder

Peace-Giver

Hope-Giver.

My Jesus — the Beautiful One.

Come.

WHERE WILL I SIT TODAY

Where will I choose to sit today, on this August morning

that smells like a hint of fall?

I want to sit in the summer of warm beauty and hopeful sunshine.
Yes.

Will I sit with the crippling fear of an unknown September?

Fears that squeeze my already limping

but hanging-onto-hope heart.

Do I want to sit with the past staring back at me

asking questions I can't possibly answer?

Is there peace sitting alongside a river of grief flowing in my being
—

unsettled and swirling up doubts?

No.

Beautiful Lord, I want to sit with you in your peace and hope and
love.

Your lovely peaceful hope.

I need to rest beside your peaceful river of HOPE.

I long to be wrapped up in your blanket of PEACE.

I need to nestle up close to your LOVING heart, safe under your gentle wing.

I find rest there.

My heart sighs

and my eyes close.

I will sit with my Father today — loved, protected, sustained.

VANILLA

"...when you walk through the fire, you will not be burned." Isaiah 43:2

Vanilla is my favorite scent. I love the smell of baking cookies.

And the smell of my new grandson's head minutes after I heard his first cry.

Sweet smells.

A cute child at work told me one morning "Miss Joanne, you smell just like a cupcake."

I'm grinning.

But I don't love the smell of smoke and fire.

I'm not talking about the relaxing smell of an evening bonfire — that's nice.

Feet up. Marshmallows in a bag. Fireflies dancing.

I'm talking about fiery flames that destroy homes, businesses, dreams.

Ugly. Ruthless. Smelly.

I've smelled like fire and smoke while walking through the fire.

I'll never know what it was like for my "friends" Shadrach, Meshach, and Abednego, standing before an arrogant king. The stench of a fiery furnace, so close. Menacing.

Still, they stood feet planted, "I KNOW my God can deliver us from your hands, BUT if not...he is STILL GOOD."

They were BRAVE because His faithfulness and goodness

made them brave.

YES!

I imagine they were way braver than I am.

Still... He stands with me in the fire.

Beautiful — radiating life and hope and peace.

He reaches out a gentle hand and I slip mine into His.

He turns His head, eyes soft and whispers "keep walking."

Together we walk, step-by-step, through the fire.

SWIMMING

"The Lord gives strength to His people; the Lord blesses His people with peace." Psalms 29:11

Swimming with my head above water, my legs feel strong,

and I kick with ease.

I can breathe well.

No aching limbs today.

Sunshine lays warm on my shoulders.

A soft, salty breeze tickles my nose.

I smile.

These kinds of days, weeks, are my favorite.

Yes. I smile, and swim, and float along in the gentle current.

Nice. Calm. Peaceful.

I try not to look behind me.

I check for waves — for harsh outcroppings of rocks.

For strong undercurrents — like fear, trauma, or grief — that might suck me under. I don't want to see those obstacles; those mean interruptions in my calm waters.

You hear me, right?

So, I keep my eyes forward, scanning the horizon.

Keeping my focus on the beautiful lighthouse — the Giver of Light — God. Trusting Him to guide me through the waters,

to keep my legs, and my heart strong.

Full of oxygen.

Not lacking anything.

I stay in the moment, enjoying the peace, experiencing the deep oxygenating breaths.

I tread water easily — I even float on my back for a while.

I'm thankful for the peaceful day

the sunshine warming me

and the Beautiful One.

With the sun, and Son shining down,

in the calm waters, and my head above water, I smile

and swim.

UNDER THEIR STURDY ROOF

"Now faith is confidence in what we hope for and assurance about what we do not see."

Hebrews 11:1

Sunday afternoons used to be time for a drive, playing games, visiting her parents.

Practicing hymns on the piano for Sunday evening service.

Now Sundays are the day she sits at the table, sunshine laying on her shoulders, as she writes a letter to her son...in jail. I know, you're shocked.

Not half as shocked as she is, no.

It wasn't a dream she had for any of her children. Prison bars.

Lock up.

Never.

Some days she wishes she could reverse time, go back to the Sundays that her children

were all together, under their sturdy roof.

Safe, fed, loved — a bedtime story, tucked in tight.

But she can't, of course, and so she trusts her FATHER

to provide for them.

She sighs.

Today her words don't come easy, but easier than they did the last time.

What is there to say, chat about? She writes about work, making supper,

his children over to go sliding.

Daily ordinary things. Even those words, inked on a page, cause some pain.

A tear sometimes stains the page.

But she writes every week.

Words of HOPE. Of redemption.

Of God's endless supply of grace.

She writes them because she believes them.

She's LIVED them.

A double rainbow stretched across a tiny fishing village after her young husband's funeral.

HOPE.

Joy from mourning.

God's hand moving, working, redeeming, in all the moments of her life.

She reminds herself and remembers.

In the writing, her own hope solidifies, and she smiles.

She ends with an XO and a "love, Mom and Dad."

Pages are neatly folded, envelope sealed, and stamped.

HOPE — sealed in a plain white envelope, sent with a kiss and a prayer.

She has seen God redeem her own story; she knows He can redeem his.

She sits at the table, sun sinking below the hill, and she closes her eyes.

She believes.

SLOW

As my youngest daughter took off her coat, she asked me, "Mama, why does Grampy's car

go so slow?"

I just helped her, gave her a snack, and smiled.

My retired dad had just given her a ride home from his house. It's true, his little white Ford car moved very slow as it inched up our long lane.

Much slower than my minivan, yes.

But then I was a young busy mom of three, a wife, a volunteer, and a piano teacher.

My van didn't usually go anywhere slow.

My dad would sometimes remind me, "Slow down dear, you want to get home safely."

And it's not like I was ever speeding (I've never had a ticket) but I was usually in a hurry

to get to the next "thing."

The years flew by quickly, and now

my dad and mom no longer walk here,

and oh, how I miss them.

I miss their smiles and voices, their presence

and their slow car.

Now as an older, and perhaps wiser, Nana

I find that my car drives the roads,

and the highway of life,

much more slowly.

And I smile.

AS THE HUMMINGBIRD

"But those who drink the water I give will never be thirsty again. It

becomes a fresh bubbling spring within them, giving them eternal life."
John 4:14[1]

She's still here.

One of the last ones I'm thinking.

Most of her kind have already flown in search of warmer climates.

This morning she sits on my feeder.

Quietly, peacefully, unhurriedly drinking from the fake red flowers filled with food.

Sustenance.

Energy.

Rarely do I see a hummingbird just chilling out on the feeder — in no hurry.

She's been there several minutes alone — resting in between long sips.

Oh, I love her.

Her beauty and grace and agility.

Her determined grit and strength. Yes!

I'm going to miss her (and her tribe) a lot.

Soon she will fly leaving my feeder forgotten and mostly empty.

But that was the purpose of the feeder all along.

To feed the birds so they could survive, grow,

build up strength and then fly.

Soar.

Live.

It served its purpose all spring and summer long.

Jesus is the beautiful feeder who feeds me "everlasting" food and water.

Everyone who drinks from this water will never thirst again.[18]

Oh Hallelujah!

Jesus gives life, meaning, HOPE and strength for my journey.

Peace on the troubled days.

Rest for my weary heart.

Sacred relationship — His purpose.

My purpose —

To abide in Him.

To rest in Him.

To drink from the cup of life and grace He beautifully offers.

And fly in the light of His love.

POSSIBILITIES

I smiled when I saw it

stopped what I was doing

and just breathed in the moment

You see I wasn't expecting it, no

The day had been grey and windy

with snow flurries — dreary and dull

So, by late afternoon in January

I wasn't looking for it

Supper was on the stove,

the puzzle was halfway done

and the day was slowing down a bit

That's why I smiled so big

Like I had won the lottery

or spied a long-lost friend

Quietly and unassuming

it made its presence known

Loud but quiet rays

of glorious yellow sunshine

laid like a warm blanket

on my hardwood floor

It lit up my somber dining room

and kissed the blooming yellow tulips

on my table

My house came alive with a soft amber glow

I sighed and breathed it in

and snapped a picture

I hadn't even considered

the possibility

that the sun would announce

itself so delightfully

I'm so thankful that it did

Thank you, Lord, for surprising possibilities

Like seeing the sun

and feeling it's warmth

and glowing in it's beautiful light

when days and seasons

are otherwise dull and grey

Possibilities are endless

when my good, good Father walks with me.

I'M FINE

"He will cover you with his feathers, and under his wings you will find refuge." Psalm 91:4

I reply I'm fine when asked how I'm doing.

Just fine.

Pretty good I say.

I mean I do All. The. Things.

I get up and get ready for work.

Wear a smile. Talk the talk.

Walk the balance beam.

I do everything I've been told to do to be *well*.

Well enough.

Stay in the Word.

Pray and praise.

Exercise regularly.

Eat healthy (mostly).

See a counselor.

Don't isolate.

Stand on one foot, balancing a teacup between my teeth (not really) but you get the point.

And yet.

Yet.

Grief is my companion for a lot of days.

The aching squeezes my chest.

Fear crawls in bed beside me — even when I try to kick him out, cover my head, and hide.

He's sneaky and mean.

Sometimes the bleeding aching hits me out of nowhere — like a sucker punch — in a store,

at work, driving the car, or washing dishes.

I have a hunch you know what I'm talking about.

If we sat together, you could tell me how you feel the same way sometimes, for different reasons but you know."

I feel your ache.

You've said it, and I've said it.

"I'm fine. I am."

And sitting here in the gentle afternoon breeze, I remember what I KNOW.

In the remembering peace settles — soft and soothing on my being.

My "fine" being.

"Trust me," He says.

Let me be your hope in the "fine."

So, I give it over to Him, Healer of bleeding hearts and broken lives.

Precious Redeemer.

Hope-Giver.

Abba.

I know that He knows it all — the past, present, and future.

And He holds it all, just like He holds me.

Resting in Him, I'm fine.

As I Walk, I Imagine

"Therefore, since we are surrounded by such a great cloud of witnesses, let us throw off everything that hinders and the sin that so easily entangles. And let us run with perseverance the race marked out for us, fixing our eyes on JESUS..." Hebrews 12:1-2

I love walking. I used to love running, a few years ago. Lacing up the sneakers, hitting the road—exhilarating (most of the time). Hubby loves to walk, too, and our daughters.

In fact, most of our family loves walking and/or running. We're walkers through and through. Snow, freezing temps, wind, and showers don't usually stop us. There's a built-in desire to "go"—walk it out, breathe the fresh air, clear my head. You probably "get it" to some degree. It's healing and restorative, right?? Borderline addictive.

They say that walking is good for your physical, mental, and emotional health. It increases your cardiovascular fitness (good for the heart), strengthens your bones, benefits your brain, helps maintain a healthy weight, and boosts muscle power and endurance. It increases serotonin and decreases the risks of many diseases including cancer. Yes!

They don't have to try to convince me—I'm sold on it! I can testify to the many benefits of walking. I imagine you can, too. I know I need good walking shoes and proper attire. I enjoy walking on the

Neck Road where I live. The beauty is spectacular, and the neighborhood walkers are friendly. There are so many roads I could walk on—so many trails and paths: the Fundy trail, Irving nature park, and Q-Plex trails. Some are narrow, others wide. Most around here have hills—some of them steep and long. Some trails are rocky and uneven and even slippery.

Hubby and I walked a "trail" up the Beehive Mountain in Acadia National Park years ago—we were terrified. We had friends guiding us who knew the way (I won't name names, but you know WHO you are) and yet we still felt unsure of our footing and afraid at times. Thankfully, we also hiked amazingly beautiful, less terrifying trails there, too, and want to return someday.

I love following the Guide as I walk. He leads me in the right path. Always.

He's even given me a "guided map" that shows me which path to walk on. The safest path—although not usually the "easy" path. When I keep my eyes on Him, the all-knowing, life-giving Leader, I walk with confidence. If I falter, He picks me up. When I'm injured, He tenderly heals me, and bandages the blisters on my tired, aching feet. Feet aching, bleeding and worn out, by rocky, harsh paths. Aching, weary hearts, too—He breathes into them his Holy oxygen. Jehovah-Rapha—beautiful Healer. He sees me. He gently takes my hand and walks beside me, holding me steady.

Jehovah-Jireh—my Provider, giving me strength to keep moving.

Daily, He is my Portion. I know I can trek the journey when He is beside me.

Determined to finish the race—I walk on.

DRIVE

"...and blessed is the one who trusts in the Lord." Proverbs 16:20

A quiet Sunday afternoon drive.

A "get a vanilla soft serve at Dairy Queen" drive.

A holding hands with my hubby of 34 years drive. Yes. Nice.

Sometimes the scenery is beautiful, in a relaxing kind of way. Ocean waves, evergreen trees, eagles soaring overhead, fall leaves waving in brilliant hues of oranges, reds, and gold.

Peaceful and pleasing.

Other times the "drive" is reckless, hazardous, and unnavigable.

Yikes, not so pleasant to the heart, eyes, or soul.

These drives lead us through valleys, dark shadows and on rugged paths. Crisis, grief, or pain (or all three) meet us around every bend. I don't love these drives so much. I'm speaking from experience here. These drives can leave me limping, scared, and tired.

The good news (I mean GREAT NEWS) is that I know the driver. Intimately.

I trust Him.

He keeps the wheel steady and the car on the road. My Father.

He takes my hand when the drive is just "too much."

He looks at me and whispers softly, "You can trust me."

He reminds me that He will get me safely to my destination and will never leave my side. Amazing love!

I trust the beautiful Driver on the drive.

Hallelujah.

DESERVE

"But God demonstrates his own love for us in this: while we were still sinners, Christ died for us." Romans 5:8

Webster's dictionary defines "deserve" as a verb meaning "to be worthy of, to earn."

I deserve a piece of chocolate cake after eating healthy all week.

I deserve a raise considering how hard I work at my job.

I deserve a day of rest after a long busy week.

I deserve... (you fill in the blank).

We live in a world that says "I deserve..."

There's a culture of entitlement. Right?

Even without the attitude of "entitlement" there's also the idea of "fairness."

Fair says that something should look like I want it to look or be what I feel it should be.

But I know all too well that "fair" and "deserve" don't get the fairness they deserve.

Life seems very upside down at times, not fair at all.

I'm thankful every day that God doesn't give me what I deserve—instead He offers grace and mercy to me...and you. My sin says I deserve punishment, but His sacrifice, death, and resurrection (Hallelujah) say I am forgiven and free. Amazing!!

It makes me want to dance and sing and shout.

He is SO good for not giving me what I deserve, but instead grace, His unmerited favor.

Yes! I'm dancing now!

THE PEPSI AISLE

I turned the corner and there she stood,

waiting in the Pepsi aisle.

Purse in hand, pushing a cart.

I met her eyes and we smiled — friends reunited

in the grocery store.

Our hearts embraced, even though our arms could not.

No matter, a heart hug is

better than any other kind

on a gray chilly November morning.

We talked about life's "goings-on"

and about the hard things, too.

It's ok, neither of us are scared to say the words,

because we've traveled this road

together for a long time now.

Weeks, months, and years have beautifully turned into

a melding and blending of hearts.

Heart aches

heart-joys

tears and prayers.

Heart-felt prayers.

Nothing too big

or too small

for a prayer spoken across a phone

or a living room

or a hospital room.

As she waited for her water

we had church in the Pepsi aisle.

"Church," you say?

On an ordinary Tuesday morning,

with no organ or choir or preacher?

Yes, church.

She preached and I said, "Hallelujah!" and raised my arm.

Yes, I did.

Twice, in fact, and said, "Come, Lord Jesus."

Oh, and you know the most beautiful part? He did.

He does.

Yes, He does.

The Beautiful One.

He meets two friends in the shopping aisle,

with busy shoppers hustling by,

and employees stocking shelves.

While toddlers are being pushed

in carts by their mothers and

a man stands beside a Salvation Army kettle.

With a radio playing on the store's loudspeakers.

He shows up even then, especially then.

Especially then!

To encourage the tired and sometimes afraid hearts

of sister-friends

of loyal hand-holders

tear-catchers and prayer warriors.

Church in the Pepsi aisle

on an ordinary Tuesday,

you better believe it.

Joy. To. The. World.

Joy to the world, the Lord is come

Oh Hallelujah — He has come!

Look up

look around

Emmanuel —

He is here

HE IS HERE

Emmanuel — God with us.

Hallelujah!

A WORD FOR THE YEAR

"Trust in the Lord with all your heart and lean not on your own under-standing, in all your ways submit to him, and He will make your paths straight." Proverbs 3:5-6

A word for the year...I started picking one a few years ago.

A word to ponder and live by for twelve calendar months.

A couple of years ago I picked "surrender."

An easy word for the lips but a bit trickier for the heart.

Did I really know how to live it? I thought I did.

I knew the song, "I Surrender All."

I could recite it verse by verse from memory. Lovely words full of meaning with a call to challenge me.

Sloughing through the trench of pain and trauma—the word became a prayer.

Lord, help me surrender. All of it—the pain, grief, aching heart, fear.

And shame—oh the dreadful shame.

I practiced raising one arm high in worship. Then gradually I added the other one.

Both hands reaching (sometimes on tiptoe) for a healing touch from heaven.

From the beautiful One who knows my every ache.

He whispers, "Not forgotten."

Or abandoned. Never.

Lovingly held and lifted up.

Feet on solid ground—firm on a foundation of HOPE.

And don't forget—dancing.

The act of surrender with arms stretched wide opened the chasms in my heart to be filled with hope, healing, mercy, and amazing astounding LOVE.

A sacred act of worship, lifting Him, lifting me.

Holy ground in my kitchen, on my walk, in the car.

Yes.

Arm lifted in the car.

I surrender all.

A TINY SPARK

A tiny spark

can bring a fire back to flames

Throw in some paper

and stir up the coals

and soon the wood stove

is radiating warmth

on a blustery sub-zero January day

A flaming fire can cook a meal

warm fingers and toes

and bring light into a dark night

Faith and hope are like that, too —

A tiny spark of faith can grow into

arms wide open in surrender

into hands lifted high in praise

even in the storm

A tiny spark of hope

can make tired feet dance

and bring healing to a wounded heart

If you look closely

you will notice sparks of joy

all around this sometimes-grey world

I'm looking for sparks of JOY

FAITH and HOPE

What sparks you?

CANZONAE DELLA TERRA

(sing with the earth and her songs)

Settled in Colors

"Yet I am always with you; you hold me by my right hand. My flesh and my heart may fail, but God is the strength of my heart, and my Portion forever." Psalms 73:23,26

Like I knew she would, Fall has arrived

Settled in with her colors of red, gold, and orange.

The view out my window is muted now

not vibrant like summer.

The grass in the river is golden

not emerald.

The hills wear a warm quilt of soft oranges, red and gold, too.

Fall's nostalgic beauty calls to me,

inviting me to embrace and enjoy the calm beauty.

It reminds me — again — to slow down and rest.

Yes, rest.

Glorious summer is a picture in the rear-view mirror.

Her spontaneous days are spent —

the frolicking summer breezes wave, *Goodbye, dear friend.*

So long 'til next July.

Leaving her memories of joyful laughter and sunshine beaches

in my mind's photo album.

If I'm being honest a bit of dread sits in part of my heart today.

A quiet (and sometimes loud) intruder.

Fears of October, November, December...sit beside the dread.

I try to ignore it

pretend it isn't there

and smile.

Intruders don't take too kindly to being ignored, so I know I have to acknowledge it.

I see it and accept it.

Speak it out loud in the quiet.

And then I speak His name —

Jehovah

Abba, Daddy

Healer

Beautiful One

and I welcome Him

arms stretched wide

heart wide open

into the quiet stillness.

My God is bigger than dread's voice.

My Father

He speaks over it

hushes it

calms it

and whispers "trust and rest."

Rest and trust — beloved daughter

Slip your hand in mine

and we will walk together

strong together

into Fall.

ACORNS

"Every good and perfect gift is from above, coming down from the Father of heavenly lights, who does not change like shifting shadows." James 1:17

River water lapped soft on the shore as I stood waiting.

Two pretty kayaks sat at the water's edge, soaking up warm afternoon rays of sun.

A duck quacked and another answered — mother and daughter maybe?

"You should come to the book club," my friend suggested.

The book called *Shades of Light*[19] was the focus of our reading and discussions. It was all a bit much as I was living in the 'angst' of a son with mental health issues, now I was going to read a book about it too?

I wasn't so sure...

As we dove into the book, one of the main characters (a mom I could relate to) talked about acorns, and how they represented God's sustaining power, His protection, and His love.

Cool, I thought. That's neat.

Well, as I stood alone on the riverbank waiting for my husband, I heard a noise.

A plop.

I turned around and looked, walking closer. A huge oak tree stood on the riverbank,

reaching over the water.

An acorn fell. Then another. Then it started to "rain" acorns!

For real (and I'm smiling big as I write this now).

Plop-plop-plop.

Acorns raining into the still water and sand beside me.

So, I did the only thing I knew to do. I gathered them up by the handful and stuffed them in my hoodie pocket. I couldn't believe it was raining acorns, and I was the only one there to watch!

I giggled.

When hubby came back, I told him, and showed him, laughing at the extravagant gift God had given me.

Loved, sustained, protected.

Bulging pockets of acorns to prove it.

In the midst of heartache, trial and limping, a miracle of love.

I do believe in miracles, and the lavish, wondrous beauty of God's heart.

If you come to my house, maybe for a night of macrame, you will see my miraculous

beautiful acorns sitting on my windowsill, reminding me to re-member — God.

MY HEART, LIKE AN OVERRIPE PEACH

"There is a time for everything, and a season for every activity under the heavens." Ecclesiastes 3:1

"Your right hand has held me up. Your gentleness has made me great. You enlarged my path under me, so my feet did not slip. The Lord lives! Blessed be my ROCK!" Psalm 18:35-36,46

On summery August mornings I can smell, see, and hear the signs of fall.

Fallen leaves, honking geese, and crickets singing abound.

I used to really love fall, but now I accept it with less fervor. Chunky pumpkins, brilliant leaves in shades of gold and red, an afternoon of apple picking, a warm breeze with a hint of chill, these traits of fall still have my heart.

An evening walk that smells of wood fires makes me smile and feel a warmth in my chest. Fall evokes warm, cozy, even nostalgic feelings, all enjoyable to my five senses. I take it all in...

Sometimes I look at old photo albums and see my children's younger faces smiling back at me from September, back-to-school photos. I fondly remember new backpacks and lunchboxes lined up, overflowing with new pencils and scribblers, waiting for the first day of school. In my mind's eye I see pony-tailed children waving at me from yellow school bus windows, and I try to smile through the sadness.

When I smell my Thanksgiving turkey baking, I see my mom donned in her apron, fluttering around her tiny kitchen. She loved cooking for us, and we loved eating her delicious meals of turkey dinner, pumpkin pie, and hot apple pie—flavors of Fall.

Even though Fall marked a season of tragedy in my life, it didn't completely hide all the beautiful attributes of the season. Grief and the sting of loss usually held a place in my heart in September, but overall light (happiness) and peace shone down on me.

Grief can make you look at memories through a foggy, tear-stained lens—some days.

I remind myself that it's ok to feel both happy and sad at the same time. Both emotions can co-exist in a girl's heart. One doesn't have to negate the other to accept the other...to experience the other.

I do feel a lot of nostalgia during the Fall months when Thanksgiving arrives and the hush of darker days settles. Yes. After all, my grown children no longer live with me, and my parents no longer walk the earth.

There's a restlessness in my spirit when Fall arrives, displaying her red, orange and gold hues like a beautiful cape. Her crown adorned with sunflowers, acorns, gourds, and leaves. I feel a bit of dread because of the shorter days, less sunshine, and chillier winds.

(I'm not a wimp, I can chin-up, dress-up, and go for a walk in the darker colder days. And I do!)

Has the grief and pain of slogging through deep "wintry valleys" made this heart of mine more fragile and tender?

Squishy—like an overripe peach? More apt to want to isolate and hide away?

Perhaps.

Spring and summer just seem more kind, gentle and life-giving to a tired limping girl like me—and maybe like you, too. See, I know that right on the heels of Fall is winter—and for me walking in that season seems to weigh me down. Darker days, longer nights, and bitter cold winds all take a toll on this hanging-onto-hope girl.

I seem to need more light than winter can give. More hope, peace, and joy than a freezing February day provides.

In these days I remember that I need to "remember God."

The word REMEMBER is spelled out in wooden scrabble letters on my windowsill. A daily reminder for my forgetful mind to remember His faithfulness.

He is in ALL things, ALL ways, *ALL* seasons.

Seasons of loss, grief, and tears that fall like cold icy rain in January. Yes—even then—*especially* then.

My windowsill always holds written scripture. I memorize hopeful truth- filled Bible verses, and I stand in my kitchen with arms lifted high and sing. Sing to Him, my Beautiful Healer, Hope-Giver, Promise-Keeper, Comforter, and Abba Father.

I speak what I know, what I believe in my heart, and I claim His truths over my life and the people I love. My people who live near, far, and in the deepest place in my mother-heart.

He is a million times faithful.

He is the good in all the good I see.

He is the holiest Holy One who resides with us.

He is the Father who holds my tiny hand in His strong gentle one.

He offers PEACE in winter, JOY in troubled times, and LOVE on the unlovely roads I sometimes traverse.

He is the lifter of my head on dark winter nights.

He always gives life to my tired "winter" soul.

I can lean on Him.

I don't have to fear the changing seasons because I know that even in "fall"

I can stand.

MY HEART AGREES WITH THE TREES

"Yes, my soul, find rest in God, my hope comes from him." Psalm 62:5

The morning,

it's cold

crunchy

frosty

shimmery with ice crystals

Frost — it lays like a chilly blanket on the farmer's field

asleep for the winter now

Resting

Silent

The colors of fall are faded,

muted.

Trees are still doggedly holding onto a bit of fall's

majestic beauty and warmth —

even in the frosty chill of a November morning

Peeks of golden leaves surprise my view

Sunshine glances through the clouds

a whisper of warm hope

It all makes me ache a little,

want to hide a little —

or much.

My heart agrees with the trees,

feeling icy

but hanging onto colors of beauty

And hope

Always hope

Beauty and hope

Even when winter is just around the corner,

her frosty hand beckoning me

Yes, even then — Hope

I stand in the kitchen and gaze at the misty

frost-kissed river grasses

My eyes are drawn to the rays of sunshine inviting a warm glow

onto the frosted picture

A thousand thoughts and memories threaten to overwhelm me

Fear waits in the corner chair

Doubt sits on my shoulder

Grief lurks in the closet

My aching heart skips a beat or two

In the silence

I hear His quiet gentle voice — again

I'm here, daughter

I AM here.

I AM

Trust my heart

Hold my hand

I'm holding yours

Lay your tired head on my shoulder

And so I do

I do

For the thousandth time this year

this month

this week

I do.

In the quiet — I do

Abba

Daddy

Beautiful One

Beautiful tear-catcher

Beautiful hand-holder

Beautiful Healer

Abba

I rest in Him

I rest on His word

I lay my head on my Father's strong

safe shoulder

And I place my HOPE in Him

I do

THE FIRST SNOW

It's the first real snowstorm of winter.

Wild winds and blowing snow

with a northerly bite.

As she putters, and puzzles and pauses

she feels a restlessness building inside.

Even though she fights it

prays against it and yes,

sometimes gives into it.

It hangs around like an uninvited guest.

A bossy rude intruder telling her how she feels.

Reminding her of painful pain

and lingering loss. Ouch.

She stands at the bedroom window,

pushes aside the curtain,

and tries to peer into the darkness.

But a pattern of icy snowflakes

is frozenly plastered to the window,

and her view is blocked.

She can only see a faint swirling of blustery snow

in the darkness outside.

She misses the sun,

longs for it like an old familiar friend.

An ache sits heavy in her chest,

and she turns away

a weak prayer on her lips.

Help, she whispers.

Somehow, the dark cold

icy snowstorms bring to the surface

grief triggered by loss,

emptiness that erases a smile,

and a weariness in her bones.

She returns to the counter stool

and sits beside a puzzle she's working on.

It's a distraction from the dread

and a relief for a moment

from the restlessness.

She tries to stay out of her head.

Her heart aches with unshed tears.

Just let them fall she tells herself

you'll feel better.

But no, she swallows them back.

Maybe tomorrow she will stand at the window letting in peeks of frozen sunshine

and let a few tears slide.

Maybe.

They say it helps, and it's healthy,

so it's good to let them fall.

To cry out a waterfall of salty tears

to release the "gunk" inside.

She thinks to herself,

Maybe tomorrow I'll wake up

and the aching grief

will be gone —

buried away for another day.

Until then she does what she knows to do.

She knows Who to trust

and Who to lean on

in the unknowing.

She leans on her Father and

rests on His promise of faithfulness

of mercy and kindness and hope.

She lays her head down to rest

with the firm belief

in His unchanging favor and

unfathomable love upon her head

and over her weary heart.

In the frozen January snowstorm

in the valley.

He IS.

DECEMBER ROAD

"When Jesus spoke again to the people, he said, 'I am the light of the world. Whoever follows me will never walk in darkness but will have the light of life.'" John 8:12

She walks along the familiar road

on a sunny December afternoon.

The sun shines down

like an old friend

whispering reminders of summer days.

As she turns the corner

and the breeze stills

she unzips her coat a little

and opens her scarf.

She smiles and prays and walks on

one step at a time.

Firmly

steadily

but not rushing.

A chickadee's song fills her ears with a simple sweet melody.

Geese honk in the distance

and slushy snow squishes

beneath her hikers.

In the quiet

She thinks of those she loves

their faces come alive in her thoughts.

Some of them are in vivid color,

some are black and white,

and others are blurry

as seen through a curtain of tears.

December always does this to her.

The nostalgic season breathes

memories to life

in a tangible way.

As she walks, she hears the voices

of her three young children —

two girls and a boy.

Two with brown eyes

one with green.

A video with sounds of laughter

singing

and even squabbling

plays in her mind.

It's as real as if it was recorded this morning.

A young father sits on the floor with them

and patiently assembles doll houses

and helps build Lego airplanes.

Boney M sings "Feliz Navidad" in the background.

The Christmas tree lights sparkle in the late afternoon shadows.

Another picture replays her mom stirring something on the stove

while wearing her Christmas apron

and her dad tries to steal a kiss from the most

beautiful woman he knows — her mom, of course.

At a family dinner on Christmas Eve, cousins dramatically act out plays, and

grandparents smile with pride.

Some of these beautiful people no longer walk here with us.

But their love shines in us

through us

and around us — especially in the

days of December.

Their love beats in our hearts

and ours in theirs

because love is eternal.

And woven through it all —

the faces

the hearts

and the memories

is the red thread of His love

binding us all together

in Him.

The Beautiful One

His love weaves us together —

those here with us

those who aren't

and those who wander.

A wayward tear slides down her chilly cheek

as she walks on to her little home.

Then she smiles

because she knows

Love still lives there,

LOVE still lives here,

In her

In her family and

In her memories.

December reminds her again that

there is LIGHT in the dark

Immanuel

God with us

Here with us

He brought His love to her

to them

to all of us.

A thrill of HOPE the weary world rejoices!

WAITING FOR A PRESENCE

Advent invites me to open

my heart

eyes

and arms

wide to receive

To ready myself in a surrendered posture

Head back

arms up

heart wide open

Heart wide open to

receive the King of Kings

Come, Lord Jesus

I wait for you this grey November morning

I long for your Presence

and your presents

of grace

HOPE

peace and JOY.

Like Mary I open my child — like heart to receive the wonder

of your beauty and light.

Light that humbly extends itself to the darkness of this world.

Like the shepherds

I bow in humble adoration

of the majestic king of kings.

I sing with the angels "glory to God in the highest."

Holy is your name

HOLY

Immanuel

God with us

God. With. Us.

God with us in our grief

and fear

and painful pain.

Oh, how beautiful those words

How my heart is overwhelmed

by the beautiful gift You are

Beautiful One

Gentle Savior

Healer and Hope-Giver

Shine your LIGHT

and HOPE

and PEACE

into my world

into our world

this first Sunday of Advent

I wait for You

I welcome You

Come, Lord Jesus

CHRISTMAS BOYCOTT

"The choir's singing carols

Bells are ringing, streets are bright

It's Christmas all around me

So why is Christmas hard to find?

December snow is falling down like I am to my knees

I could use some hope right now

'Cause right now hope is hard to see

Help me still believe

For God so loved this broken world

He sent His only Son

To a carpenter and a teenage girl

To show us all His love

He left His home in heaven

To make Heaven my home

My Emmanuel is with me

And I'll never be alone

Down here my heart can't find much to believe in

But I still believe in Christmas."[20]

Can Christmas be boycotted?

I like to think so. I want to know so.

Is that even a "thing"?

I want to think so.

I need to believe it.

I long to hold it tightly and believe in the possible reality.

The real possibility.

Boycott maybe isn't the perfect word for my desire.

It's not that I don't like

or even love Christmas.

I do.

I love all the traditions and feelings

and gift exchanges and the meaning and warmth that sits alongside them.

I do, truly.

Christmas used to be my favorite.

Wrapping, baking, decorating, hiding gifts, surprising loved ones.

Family.

And celebrating the most beautiful gift, Jesus.

Beholding the most beautiful treasure of the humble babe in a manger.

Mary, Joseph, baby — family.

Carols, choirs, pageants, nativities, concerts, and communion.

Family.

Turkey dinners and pumpkin pie.

Strings of soft glowing lights.

Ganong chocolates and crunchy chicken bones galore.

Red velvet dresses and plaid bow ties.

And family.

So maybe what I really want is to avoid it.

Side-step December.

Bury my head 'til January.

Yes.

Because loss equals pain equals wanting to avoid.

Avoidance.

Loss avoidance.

Instead of wanting to avoid it, couldn't I learn to make peace with it

somehow?

I mean that's what Jesus came for, didn't He?

To bring peace? hope? *presence?*

Peace and hope are His gifts to us.

Oh how we need them.

Oh how *I* need them.

Especially in the pain and loss and hurt.

Peace in the pain.

Hope in the hurt.

Love sitting with loss.

Emmanuel — God with us.

Offering His presence.

Offering His presents.

God with me.

God with you.

God with me and you in the pain.

And with the lost and broken and sad.

The sadly broken.

I'll hold onto the babe in the manger who arrived with gifts — of salvation, mercy, kindness, and love,

PEACE and HOPE.

I'll lay down my "avoidance"

and my broken heart

and let Him heal me.

His arms stretched wide — to offer the most beautiful gift of saving grace — invite me to open my arms wide to receive Him.

Arms wide open.

To surrender the painful hurt and brokenness to the Beautiful Healer.

To surrender *avoidance*.

To receive and welcome the Beautiful Holy babe.

So, with my eyes and heart solely focused on Him,

I will welcome the season of Advent wonder

and the Hope-giving Babe.

Babe of Mary

Gentle Savior

Come sweet baby – Emmanuel – **the Beautiful One**

into my world.

Into OUR world.

With an open heart I welcome You.

Come.

THE FIRST DAY OF DARK DECEMBER

On this first day of dark December

shine your light into my world

into our world

Into the darkness of a thousand tears

Into the weight of heaviness

Into bleeding hearts

and tired aching feet

Shine your light —

your beautiful

unstoppable LIGHT

Help me to see You

hear You

sense Your peaceful Presence

Help me hold tightly to Your hand

while you hold tightly to mine

to ours

Shine HOPE

Shine PEACE

Shine unfathomable LOVE

into my world,

into our world

Shine Lord Jesus

With outstretched arms

and an open heart

I welcome You

HIBERNATE IN HIS GOODNESS

"But the angel said to them, 'Do not be afraid. I bring you good news that will cause great joy for all the people. Today in the town of David a Savior has been born to you; he is the Messiah, the Lord. This will be a sign to you: You will find a baby wrapped in cloths and lying in a manger.'" Luke 2:10-12

As the darkness of December

settles in,

I remind myself

He is GOOD.

He is STILL good.

Yes, when all the world goes dormant,

we hibernate in his goodness.

He is always good.

In my heart I know it.

My heart agrees with His

that He is good,

in all ways,

at all times, He is good.

Even if

and even if not,

He is still good.

When I can

and even when I can't,

He is good,

so good.

So good to me.

A thousand times my heart sings it.

Yes! He is good!

In the darkness and in the light,

In the knowing and unknowing,

In the longing and surrender,

He is kind and good.

When I lay my head on soggy pillow

and wake in the dark before dawn,

He whispers goodness.

In all the wrapping and unwrapping

He comes wrapped in swaddling cloths as the Savior of the world.

He sings grace and kindness over me.

Where would I be

without His goodness and love?

Immanuel.

Here with me.

Here with us.

A thrill of HOPE.

The WEARY world rejoices

in His goodness.

ADVENT LONGINGS

"Come, let us bow down in worship, let us kneel before the Lord our Maker; for he is our God and we are the people of His pasture, the flock under His care." Psalm 95:6-7

Beautiful One

this Advent season we are so aware

of our need for you.

Our longing for you

Our hoping for you

Our hoping IN you

Immanuel

here with us

God with us

Bring your peace into our pain

Bring your healing

and HOPE

into our hurt

Bring your grace into our grief

We invite you

to sit with us in

our aching longing,

our longing aching.

We long for you to speak truth

into our unspoken longings

We ask for your help

in our helplessness

and HOPE in

our hopelessness

Come like the soft breath

of a mother's lullaby

Come like the strong hand

of a gentle father

Lead us with

the kind hand

of a good shepherd.

Come gently kind Savior

We invite you into our worlds

today and every day

Come Beautiful One

We welcome

and ADORE You

On bended knee we welcome you.

HE IS PEACE

"For to us a child is born, to us a son is given, and the government will be on his shoulders. And he will be called Wonderful Counselor, Mighty God, Everlasting Father, Prince of Peace."

Isaiah 9:6

We're all searching for peace

all of us I'm sure

I'm searching for peace

this December — this year

But here's the thing —

peace as a feeling

as a "thing" to be grasped

and longed for

and hoped for

is elusive, unreliable, and finicky

complicated and unstable.

Here is the good news

the GOOD NEWS

Peace is a Person

He's the most Beautiful One

the Holy One

Isaiah prophetically named him

the Prince of Peace

He is eternally present

He is unwaveringly reliable

He is a firm foundation

He is completely sure

and stable in all ways.

Immanuel

He brings peace

He whispers peace

He declares peace

when grief sit heavy on my "not so fine being"

and when doubt shouts despair!

And when fear locks its grip on me

He holds out His hands

and gently says,

"Come sit with me, I'll give you my peace."

He whispers, "I know you're not so fine, but you're beautifully mine."

His peace is like the sun

that warms my face

and shines it's LIGHT

on my December afternoon walk.

Steady, sure, real, unchanging.

Peace — I look for Him

I long for Him

and He walks with me.

Peace.

CHRISTMAS IN PLASTIC TOTES

"He will cover you with his feathers, and under his wings you will find refuge; his faithfulness will be your shield and rampart." Psalm 91:4

"The Word became flesh and made his dwelling among us. We have seen his glory, the glory of the one and only Son, who came from the Father, full of grace and truth." John 1:14

To be honest it's early for me, and I usually wait until closer to New Years, but this year I feel more than ready. I'm taking down all the decorations, ornaments, and lights, and packing them away until next December.

My pretty white ceramic angels get carefully wrapped and placed in just the right spot. Handmade by my mom for me many Christmases ago, they hold a special place in my heart and home.

A simple wood-carved nativity rests quietly in the tote beside the delicate angels. The angels will wait until their moment next fall to draw attention to the humble manger scene...when they sit on my favorite shelves once again. Pretty white lighted houses, snowball garlands, twinkly lights and advent candles all get gently packed away for another season.

Even though I've loved having them around me this season, I'm ready to move forward into a new year.

I wonder as I carefully set "Christmas" back into plastic totes, am I packing away JOY, PEACE, and HOPE, too?

Is the humble babe born to be our Savior, Redeemer, Hope-Giver, and Light also being placed in a cold tote in a dark closet?

"May it never be so," I pray quietly.

When January soon bites with the hard cold frost, and when the shortened days with lingering nights leave me restless, can I look for and find JOY?

Does PEACE settle around me like a warm soft cloak, enveloping my limping heart with a cushioned wall of protection?

Is HOPE what I cast my eyes toward when I bundle up and venture out on my frosty walk by the river?

I'm reminded of a familiar verse I had chalked onto my board last year "Be joyful in hope, patient in affliction, faithful in prayer."[21] Oh yes, I remember, and I breathe deep breaths. I remind myself once again to practice being "joyful in hope" as I lean into my Father. My hope is in Him, and in His steady faithfulness to me, not in my circumstances. My emotions, moods, and circumstances are ever changing, but He is constant, unmoving, and ever faithful.

I close my eyes and feel the Beautiful One take my hand, walking me into a new year. Joy, peace, hope, and faith are brilliantly alive in me because He dwells in my heart. He doesn't walk away now that Christmas is a memory for another year.

I smile and whisper a prayer of thanks that lays like a warm blanket over my soul—my sometimes-weary soul. His gifts are mine for the receiving, not only in December, but all year long.

I open my hands and heart to welcome Him, receive Him, and treasure His gifts.

The weary world rejoices, not only that He came, but that He lives—oh Hallelujah, He lives! That is the best GOOD NEWS ever!

As I close the door on totes full of Christmas, I walk forward in the light of Christ. I won't forget the baby born to be the Redeemer of the world.

When the darkness of this world surrounds me, and grief and pain seem like constant companions, He illuminates my pathway with joy, hope, peace, grace, and His presence.

He gives me strength for the journey and never leaves me alone.

Abba. Daddy.

Kind Savior.

Immanuel – God with me.

God with all of us.

JANUARY

"Though the fig tree does not bud...yet I will rejoice in the Lord, I will be joyful in God my Savior." Habakkuk 3:17-18

As I step into January

I wonder

what will this year look like?

The days, weeks, months

move fast

but the hours move slow.

The one-step-at-a-time walking is slow.

Slow is good and can be *really* good

because slower is quieter.

And in the quiet,

hearing comes easier.

Hearing His voice

in the slower quiet stepping.

And I wonder

will I find myself walking

on the sandy beach of my island home

with the sun warm on my face

and a hand holding mine?

Or will I walk on a colder snowy path

with frosty wind whipping my face?

Will the waves kiss my toes

and the salty air

touch my lips and tongue?

Or will my toes and fingers

get frostbite on an icy path

rugged and harsh?

I don't know.

I wonder and think and pray.

I slow down and remember.

In the unknowable January hours

I do know the WAY to walk,

I know the right path.

Yes, I know WHO to follow

with slow, steady, listening steps.

Eyes up and breathing prayers,

I trust the map

the pathway

and the Shepherd.

I step in trust.

When fear sits on my shoulder and shouts "how?"

I know the Way-Maker.

In the swirling chaos I know the Truth-Speaker.

And when hope hangs in the balance I know the Hope-Giver.

I cling to the Life-Giver.

I follow Him,

and I walk in His footsteps

as He leads the way

Into the hours, days,

weeks, and months.

Whatever the year holds

I walk with Him

into the unknown

trusting

the Beautiful Knowing One.

A Gray Expanse of Craters

"Praise him, sun and moon, praise him, all you shining stars." Psalm 148:3

"But you are a chosen people, a royal priesthood, a holy nation, God's special possession, that you may declare the praises of him who called you out of darkness into his wonderful light." 1 Peter 2:9

The moon has my love, I'll admit it...

She always has—but the love has grown stronger as I've grown older.

All the beautiful stages—full, half, quarter, crescent (fingernail)—my attention is not picky!

I especially love it when you can see the moon during the day, and I get excited almost every time I spy it in the blue sky.

So many instances of seeing breathtakingly beautiful moons flood my memory.

Many years ago, I was riding a Ferris wheel with my daughter at Old Orchard Beach, and as darkness fell a vibrant-orange full moon seemed to rise from the horizon into the navy sky. I was speechless, and I can still recall the way it made me feel.

Surreal...Amazing!

One evening while driving on the highway toward home, after visiting my dad in the nursing home, I was feeling a bit sad and nostalgic. As I drove, a large, almost unreal, brilliant harvest moon rose over a hill.

Once again, I was in awe of the moon's beauty. All other thoughts were put on hold as I took her in.

Something about it makes my heart catch a little in my chest.

Early one dark winter morning this last January as I walked into the kitchen to start the coffee, I noticed a light shining into the kitchen. When I turned around a full moon was reflecting on the river and beaming in the windows, illuminating the room. I stood by the window, quietly breathing in the beauty.

I whispered a thank you to my Father, the creator of all light.

I cling to this word, "Light."

I cling so deeply that I decided to make it my word of the year.

Not only for the connection to the moon, but also because I want to reflect on His LIGHT all year.

The moon is just one tangible reminder of His light, a reminder of the way He shines His light into my sometimes dark, dreary "winter" world. Yes!

"I'm nothing without the Son's amazing grace,

on everything I do.

If you're shining on me,

I'm shining right back for you.

I wanna be the moon,

Lord, I wanna be the moon for you."[22]

The lyrics talk about being a reflection of God—His light and majesty and beauty. The moon doesn't have its own light; it reflects the sun's light.

Ah yes!

On its own, the moon is a grey expanse of craters, rocks, and hardened lava.

It shows signs of being "knocked down," if you will. Asteroids and comets have struck the surface with such force it has left scars—large ugly ones. Ouch.

I know what that feels like, and I have a few scars to prove it. Grief, trauma, and pain have left some scars on my tender heart.

Though not as obvious as craters, I can feel them.

I'm guessing you have some, too, my friend.

The good news is, I'm here to testify that there is also beauty in the healing process.

Scars aren't my identity, and they aren't the moon's either. The moon has many admiring fans because of its ability to shine the most glorious light into dark nights. Can I get an amen?

Illuminating beauty.

Why do lovers want to sit under a moonlit sky?

Why does Bill Bailey offer to lasso the moon for his lover in the holiday classic, *It's A Wonderful Life?*

Why do people "chase" the moon?

I think it's because it feels romantic and wondrous.

Wondrous—just like the healing power of Jesus, Jehovah-Rapha, Beautiful Healer.

Healer of broken dreams and limping aching hearts. I know.

I know.

He tenderly touches the broken parts of my life and heals them. Sometimes with just a word from Him—but usually over a lengthy "walking and working it out" process.

When I lean into Him, He gives me what I need. Sometimes what I need is a counselor with a kind face speaking hope and healing over my wounds. When I surrender the hurt, He heals me—gently—like the kind, merciful Savior He is.

So, I want to be like the moon, reflecting His light to the world—craters and all—telling of His goodness, faithfulness, kindness, and beauty.

Amen and amen.

Shine!

THE SPRING CHICKADEE

"See I am doing a new thing! Now it springs up, do you not perceive it?

I am making a way in the wilderness and streams in the wasteland."
Isaiah 43:19

Hello...Spring

and hello sunshine

and pink rain boots

Hello smell of melting snow (I know you know)

Hello rippling brook singing a joyful

melody of release

Hello chickadee chirping your name

in the trees

Hello dear family who hold all of my heart

Hello friends who walk into my home bringing smiles and laughter

caring and community

Hello long amber rays of sunshine laying on my hardwood floor in
late afternoon

Hello sweet Dolly who lays with eyes closed soaking up the sun

Hello to walks with pups on the Neck Road

Hello to hugs and maskless faces and eye crinkling smiles

Hello...Spring

I welcome you

on this March day filled with potential

for growth and life and new possibilities

yes — and abundant sunny days

Son-filled days

and HOPE

SHE FINALLY BLOOMED

"I will be like the dew to Israel: he will blossom like a lily..." Hosea 14:5

She finally bloomed.

I'm so happy.

I laughed when I saw the tiny purple bud.

I showed hubby, even though he probably isn't as excited as I am.

Here's the thing...she needed more sunlight!

Friends, it was a cloudy, dark winter. Even though I set her in a spot where there "should" have been plenty of light, there was little sunshine.

That's why she didn't bloom for a long time — weeks, months.

It seemed like FOREVER.

So, a few weeks ago I moved her a bit so she could get the afternoon and evening sunshine. Oh, I knew right away that she was much happier — her leaves perked up

and turned a more brilliant green. Yes!!

So, I waited, and waited some more, and today, she has a tiny blossom.

Two, three, four, in fact!

Hallelujah! Can I get an amen?

I'm dancing a little.

She needed more sun in order to bloom,

just like I need more of the Son in order to bloom, am I right?

Yes — simple truth in an object lesson (remember those) from a pretty African violet.

Stand in His sunshine,

breathe in the light from the Son,

and bloom

HOPE!

Amen and amen

MARCH, YOU SLAY ME

March, you slay me a little

Sometimes a LOT

You March in like a lion and leave

roaring like one too

One moment you're sunny

with a hint of warmth

and the next you are ferocious and loud with a blustery bite

Should I wear my winter coat

or do I dare don my lighter layers?

When will I be able to sit on my deck in the lea

with sweet soft sunshine warming my winter-weary bones?

Will you bark with fierce teeth

or purr like a kitten, who knows?

The wind howls across my deck

knocking my bird feeder to the ground

reckless, wild, unbridled,

and then in a moment

all is quiet and fair with rays of sun

shyly peeking through gray clouds

And in it all

there's a longing in my soul

for spring and warmth

and heavenly sunshine smiles

For forsythia blooming bright yellow

and robins hopping on the front lawn

For grandchildren giggling

on an Easter egg hunt outside

and a game of hide and seek

For pitching balls to my grandson

and girls with braids riding bikes in the court

Because somehow in the unfolding of spring

hope is renewed

and tired feet feel refreshed to keep walking in hope and faith

March — you are unpredictable and cloudy, blue skies and friendly,

snarling then laughing

Freezing then warm

snowstorms and green grass

Who are you exactly?

Winter or Spring?

A conglomeration of both I suppose

and even though most days you slay me

I also welcome you

Welcome — the reluctant bearer of *Spring*

MOTHER'S DAY

Hear us, Lord, this Mother's Day,

Strengthen those who walk weary,

And hold close those who grieve

Rain your love upon the ones who "shine" with love this day.

Bless the strong ones and the weak ones,

The resting and the rushing ones.

The surrounded and the alone ones,

The empty and the filled ones.

We honor each beautiful one, Lord —

The earthly and the heavenly ones,

The healed, restored, and shining ones,

The limping, bleeding, aching ones.

Each one — treasured, beautiful, chosen...

Shine your love upon each Mother, Mom, Mama — on this their special day.

FIREFLIES AND SHORTCAKE

"The Lord loves righteousness and justice; the earth is full of his unfailing love." Psalm 33:5

Summer days and sunshine, June's full moon and the longest day.

Bird songs, a squirrel's chatter, and the buzz of a bumble bee.

Fuchsia hanging planters on the porch. Pork chops sizzling on the neighbor's barbecue.

Fireflies. Sunsets. Strawberry shortcake.

A long day at the beach with sandy toes and a sunburned nose.

Yes, summer—I sigh. I breathe it all in.

Deeply, slowly, savoring the moments so they don't race by in a blink. But they do anyway—they always do. I blink and mid-August mornings smell like a fall breeze.

But here, today, I savor all of the "summerness."

Why do I love summer so?

I don't know, except I do. It's the warm and the cheery sun and a day at the beach. My body soaks in the rays of sun—like beams of light and life. Everything in nature seems more ALIVE and well. Life's hard and heavy things seem a bit lighter, if you know what I mean. Summer seems more kind and more healthy—sweeter for the soul.

My toes curl in the warm, salty sand. My hands pick up pretty shells and small, white rocks for my collection. My chilly, aching feet wade along the freezing water's edge. Seagulls sing their crying screech against the salty breeze.

Driftwood art hangs on my wall. Sea glass necklaces adorn my neck. Pretty shells grace my nooks and crannies.

Coastal beauty—it fills me up.

Being an island girl from a tiny, rugged fishing community, raised beside beaches and wharves and creeks, I savor all the ways I can be outside in nature. Sitting there, with the sun on my head, sand in my toes, listening to the waves sing, I feel the presence of God.

His majesty speaks a thousand words I can barely whisper.

The ocean reflects His name. Rugged rocks display His handiwork.

White fluffy clouds call attention to His untouchable glory, His unspeakable gloriousness.

"The heavens declare the glory of God; the skies proclaim the work of his hands. Day after day they pour forth speech; night after night they reveal knowledge. They have no speech; they use no words; no sound is heard from them. Yet their voice goes out into all the earth, their words to the ends of the world."[23]

I see it.

I feel it.

I love it—because I love the Creator.

The Beautiful One, Maker of my heart, Keeper of my heart.

Healer of my heart, too, when my heart feels crushed and tossed about by waves of grief. He meets me with an outstretched hand. I can lean into Him when the salty tears wet my cheeks. He speaks in the soft breeze, "Be still, and know that I am God."[24]

He created my eyes to "see" and my ears to "hear" His melodies of unwavering, matchless, lavish LOVE.

Towards me—towards you.

For all of us spinning wildly around on this green and blue planet of beauty.

I sing in the summer of His LOVE.

I rest in the meadow of His PEACE.

And in His HOPE.

THE SUN BECKONS

The Light shines in the darkness and the darkness has not overcome it.
John 1:5

The Lord is my light and salvation — whom shall I fear? The Lord is the
stronghold of my life — of whom shall I be afraid? Psalm 27:1

The sun beckons to me

as I stand in the kitchen.

It smiles as it glances off the river

and shimmers a little in the bare winter trees

yes — it invites me

to come outside and play

almost like a dare said with a wink.

But it's so COLD, I say to myself — *it's frigid,*

not fit for walking today

the mercury reads — 19 degrees!

Still the invitation keeps coming,

and my feet feel a restless urge

to don their boots,

Why not try?

I tell myself

I could only walk for a bit

then return to the house

warmed by a wood fire

and rest toasty by the roaring wood stove.

Soon my coat is zippered

pink hat snugly squished onto my head

and mitts tucked into sleeves.

I open my door, and the brilliant sun welcomes me,

and I smile and squint and walk.

I try to walk slow, but that's hard for me,

so I fast walk along the road,

and soon I see peeks of the river

The smiling sun,

the frozen pewter river

and the blue sky

When I reach the top of the hill

I am winded a little and warmed.

I walk on enjoying the quiet scenic view.

I say hello to a walking neighbor

and peek at a few shy deer on a lawn.

I see the sun before me, and when I turn

— oh yes, when I turn and walk — I FEEL it.

Like a hello from a best friend

the sun's warm rays

lay like a soft blanket on my back

like a hug from an old friend,

like a love tap on the shoulder

from a brother saying,

Hey, I'm still here

I'M STILL HERE.

And again, I smile

and sneak a giggle,

and I breathe.

As I walk along the Neck

the road slopes down

and my steps almost glide

on the familiar path toward home,

I'm glad I went.

I feel refreshed,

awakened, and alive.

My lungs full with clear, life-giving oxygen

pumping blood to all my organs,

to my heart and my brain,

reminding me to remember the sun

and to remember the Son.

To remember the Beautiful One.

You knew I'd remind you

and myself

of the certainty of the sun

and the Son's certain truth —

that they are both still shining,

still giving life,

inviting us to live,

beckoning you and me

to get outside even when it feels bitter

— and I KNOW it can feel bitter.

And to keep walking,

keep believing,

keep breathing,

keep opening our arms and hearts wide.

To keep living and

keep welcoming the Son.

Even in January's

cold bitter days,

the Son is still SHINING.

He shines.

LAY LIKE THE BREATH

Beautiful One, lay like the breath of an August morning across our aching hearts.

Even in beautiful, warm summer, our broken hearts ache.

Our unspoken longings float along the sweet summer breezes.

Whispered prayers are carried along by beach waves, breaking along the sand

with the stain of tears.

Beautiful One, take our calloused hands and walk with us here in the brokenness

alongside the summer beauty of sunrises and sunsets.

Your gentle presence surrounds us when we don't know how to keep hope — walking.

We place our aching longings at your feet and ask You to help us leave them there.

Today.

Tomorrow.

Tonight - when we lay our tired heads on soggy, tear-stained pillows.

Grant us peace in the night of unrestful, restless rest.

You are our everything.

In our every heartbeat, we whisper your name, your beautiful name
— Healer,

Comforter, Hand-Holder.

Redeemer.

Abba.

Thank you for being our everything.

MOUNTAIN CLIMBED

"He will call on me, and I will answer him: I will be with him in trouble, I will deliver him and

honor him." Psalm 91:15 (read that again, BEAUTIFUL*!)*

Yesterday I climbed a huge mountain.

Yes, I did.

It was hard, really hard. I didn't know if I was going to make it.

I felt like my hikers were too big, and my backpack was weighed down

— too heavy for my small frame.

I felt like I was blindfolded — I couldn't navigate the path well.

I wasn't prepared really...no.

I felt like I couldn't get enough oxygen in my lungs,

and I feared I would fall.

I was feeling exhausted.

Blistered.

Overwhelmed and sad.

Truth is...I never left the yard.

Well, we did go for a kayak this morning — church in the kayak on the river — amazing!

I made lunch, mowed the lawn, sat on the deck enjoying the sun

and wrote a letter to my son.

Sunday is the day I write to him — hope and normalcy inked on a page.

I really didn't climb a mountain, blindfolded, and all that

but it *felt like I did.*

The weight of carrying an ache can feel like that, am I right?

It can make easy things; even easy fun things feel heavy or tiring.

I think you know what I'm talking about.

The ache may be different for you, but you KNOW.

The ache that sits in my chest like a rude intruder

won't back down some days.

Even on sunny warm days that feel amazing — yes, even then.

But Jesus — Beautiful Healer — He says "Come, rest a while."

He kindly offers to take my backpack,

the one weighed down with fear, sadness, and aching.

The heavy, weighted, stone-filled backpack.

He says I can let Him carry it.

I want to.

And to let go of the feeling that I have to carry the weight, alone.

It's too much.

So, in the front yard with the sunshine warm on my back,

tired and limping, I hand it over to Him.

His tender hands touch mine as He takes it from me.

He smiles and looks at me tenderly.

Oh, it's not heavy for Him, no.

In the giving, I feel the weight lifted.

I won't climb any more mountains today, I will rest.

Rest in His HOPE, His healing touch, and His kind, faithful Presence.

Rest — beside the Beautiful Carrier of backpacks and burdens.

EPILOGUE

COBBLESTONE DRIVE

Once upon a time 3 children lived on a Cobblestone drive

with their parents (and Kitty).

It wasn't that long ago, but it seems like it was so long ago

it could be a fairy tale, you know?

Life was easy, sunny, uncomplicated.

Weekdays meant school and activities, Friday night was pizza night,

and usually a noisy sleepover.

Sunday was church and chicken dinner in a roaster, then board games

and 4-wheeler rides.

Jesus lived with us, too — in the beauty and chaos of family living.

Ah...I remember.

An older brother with two sisters — one a brown-eyed mer-maid

and the other a green-eyed, busy bee.

Mostly they lived in harmony (but not ALWAYS)

Guitars strummed, girls giggled, skateboards clacked,

and Newsboys played on a CD player.

Pizza was eaten, lemonade sold, and Kraft Dinner was con-sumed

by hungry friends.

Ball hockey scored on nets in the basement

and Polly Pockets played silly in the kitchen.

Days raced by

and moments melted into years.

Slow, but fleeting — ordinary yet magical days.

The mom and dad wondered if the days would ever end,

and then they did.

They stood proud as graduation caps were pinned on

and as the children tested their wings to fly.

They flew.

One girl flew on a love song to the prairies -— light and pretty.

Another girl captured beautiful memories

and turned them into exquisite photo mosaics.

Two beautiful twirling tornadoes of light.

One boy, he studied and planted

and got lost in a world he was trying to find.

Trying so hard but losing.

Twirling in a lost world.

The mom and dad sit in an empty nest and remember.

Reflect on the days lived a few decades ago.

Smiles, tears, laughter, prayers — all mixed together

in a swirly concoction of memories.

Three things remain: *"faith, hope, love,*

and the greatest of these is LOVE."[25]

All are held together by a loving Father — Father of them all —

the ones called Mom, Dad,

son, sister, and little sister.

And it's not a fairy tale — it's a Love Story

written in grace,

blood and redemption.

By His amazing mercy and kindness,

He is still writing their stories.

1. "Something Beautiful," William J. Gaither and Gloria Gaither. Copyright © 1971 HannaStreet Music (BMI) (adm.at Capitol CMGPublishing.com) All
rights reserved. Used by permission.

2. Isaiah 41:13, NIV. All Bible verses are from the New International Version (NIV) unless otherwise specified.

3. Copyright © 2013Thankyou Music Ltd (PRS) (adm.worldwide@CapitolCMGPublishing.com excluding the UK & Europe which is adm@IntegratedRights.com) All rights reserved. Used by permission.

4. Public Domain

5. "Goodness of God," Bethel Music, 2018.

6. 1 Thessalonians 5:16-18.

7. Isaiah 41:13.

8. "Gratitude," Nichole Nordeman, Copyright © 2002 Ariose Music (ASCAP) (adm.at CapitolCMGPublishing.com) All rights
reserved. Used by permission.

9. Ann Voskamp, One Thousand Gifts: A Dare to Live Fully Right Where You Are, Zondervan, 2010.

10. annvoskamp.com

11. Patricia Raybon, Take Heart: 100 Devotions to Seeing God When Life's Not Okay, Revell, 2020.

12. Isaiah 46:4.

13. Proverbs 13:12, The Good News translation.

14. Ann Voskamp, The Broken Way: A Daring Path into the Abundant Life, Zondervan, 2016.

15. Ann Voskamp, The Broken Way: A Daring Path into the Abundant Life, Zondervan, 2016.

16. 2 Timothy 4:17.

17. New Living Translation.

18. John 4:13-14.

19. Sharon Garlough Brown, Shades of Light: A Novel, IVP Books, 2019.

20. "I Still Believe in Christmas," Anne Wilson, Jeff Pardo & Matthew West. Copyright © 2021 Jacobs Story Music (BMI) BrentHood Music (BMI) Meaux Mercy (BMI) Capitol CMG Paragon (BMI) (adm.at CapitolCMGPublishing.com) All rights reserved. Used by permission.
21. Romans 12:12.
22. "Be the Moon," Tyler Hubbard, Chris Tomlin, & Corey Crowder. Copyright © 2020S.D.G. Publishing (BMI) Capitol CMG Paragon (BMI) (adm.at CapitolCMGPublishing.com) All rights reserved. Used by permission.
23. Psalms 19:1-4.
24. Psalm 46:10.
25. Corinthians 13:13.

Manufactured by Amazon.ca
Bolton, ON

32052243R00164